CHOOSING YOUR PSYCHIC PATHWAY

Ideas To Help Develop Your Psychic Skills

Carol Arnall

Published by Davies, Staffordshire, England.

Copyright © 2009 C. A. Arnall

www.carolarnall.com

ISBN: 978-0-9561564-5-7

Cover photograph copyright Carol Arnall 2010

Edited and formatted by Angel Editing
www.angelediting.com

ACKNOWLEDGEMENTS

To Lyn, Kathy, Nick, and everyone who contributed to the book. A huge thank you to you all, and to Hazel for your positive thinking!

Thanks also go to the Rugeley Mercury, Rugeley Post and the Express & Star for printing my appeals for ghost stories in their papers.

Angel Editing, as ever brilliant.

Other books by the author

Mystical Staffordshire
Ghostly Staffordshire
Staffordshire Hauntings
Mysterious Occurrences
Eerie Happenings
Poems and Dreams
Memories of Rugeley
Dreams Explained
Birmingham Girls
Mysterious Happenings

Fiction
Dancing with Spirits
Spirits of the Lights

Visit
www.carolarnall.com

For Hazel, my best friend

INTRODUCTION

This book gives an insight into how you can develop your psychic skills. It examines my involvement in the psychic world, and the ways and methods I discovered to help develop my psychic ability. There is a section on ghosts – including some ghostly tales that illustrate my points – tarot cards, mediums, time travel, and many more of the psychic sciences that I have discovered along the way.

There are discussions on all the above, allowing the reader to form their own opinions on whether they want to follow a particular pathway or not; it also shows how the various methods deployed by psychics may help improve their lifestyle.

For anyone who is new to the psychic world and wonders if they have psychic skills, this book can be used as a first-step introduction and will give an insight into how to proceed. There is advice on how to go about setting up as a psychic and how to avoid the pitfalls.

I have included my interpretation of the Tarot cards, dream interpretations, and other helpful suggestions as to how you can develop your psychic skills.

I have not gone into great detail with any of my ideas as I think it is far better that an individual chooses their own way of developing their skills and ideas. Too much information when a person is starting out can be confusing.

I hope the book gives the reader a clear insight into the different pathways of the psychic world.

CHOOSING YOUR PSYCHIC PATHWAY

MY STORY

I saw my first 'ghost' when I was about 7 years of age. I was walking back to school after lunch, head down looking at the floor when, for some reason or other, I glanced up. Not far ahead of me, I saw a young girl around my own age walking in the same direction. She was dressed in a similar dress to the one I was wearing. I wondered who she was.

The street was deserted apart from the two of us. I tried walking faster to catch her up, but the distance between us remained the same. Try as I might, I couldn't shorten the distance. It was strange to say the least.

I watched her intently, determined I was going to catch her up. I started to run and she promptly disappeared in front of my eyes.

I rubbed my eyes not believing that someone could disappear like that - but she had. I knew I had seen a ghost; there was no other explanation. This incident didn't frighten me at all. Despite being young, or perhaps because of it, I accepted that ghosts existed. My family would have scoffed at me if I had told them, particularly my three brothers. So I kept the 'girl ghost sighting' to myself. I never found out who she was, but I have never forgotten her.

Over the years, my interest in ghosts deepened. I read everything I could on the subject. At times, I must admit I questioned whether I had actually seen a ghost and wondered if it had been my childish imagination. Who knows? But it began a life-long interest that has never diminished.

From the time I joined the library at an extremely young age, I read any books that contained ghost stories, both fiction and non-fiction; anything that had a ghost in it was food for my soul. Films, radio programmes, magazines, anything that contained a 'ghostly reference', I had to digest.

As I grew up, I began to see other ghosts; some I recognised, others I didn't. However, asking around the family and giving descriptions of the ghosts I had seen, I would eventually discover who the ghostly apparitions were.

My research drew me to like-minded people and I would hear their fascinating stories of the ghosts they had seen. All this led me further down the path of the unexplained. The more I discovered, the more I wanted to know.

I discovered tarot cards and found they are a useful tool to help reach the 'other side', though I wouldn't recommend anyone trying this unless in the hands of a professional reader with many years of experience. The same goes for the Ouija board; this can be a highly dangerous 'game' in the wrong hands.

The majority of people who see a ghost will only ever

see the one, and others I have spoken to about their sightings are still scared many weeks down the line.

'It was such a shock,' is normally the first thing they say. I quite agree with them. If something disturbs you in the middle of the night, you may well first think you have burglars and are going to be battered to death, or you could even have a heart attack. Some ghosts have no respect for your finer feelings. After all, I should imagine there is no night or day to them. After all, they are on a higher spiritual plane than we are, or so we are told. Hence, disturbing your sleep is not going to worry them in any way whatsoever.

Of course, even if you recognise the spectre, it is still an almighty shock, but at least you have the assurance it's not a murderer standing beside your bed. What if you don't know your visitor? The first reaction, obviously, is to dive back beneath the duvet or head for the nearest exit. After all, being woken up in such an untimely manner is no joke, let alone being confronted by a ghost while you are still half-asleep. Yes, it can be scary, but if you can manage to keep calm by taking a few deep breaths and trying to stop shaking, take a peep. If the ghost hasn't disappeared by this time, I think you'll be surprised at just how ordinary the spirit will appear.

From my own experience, a ghost always looks real, but you do realise almost immediately that you are seeing a ghost. It is quite difficult to explain, but the image you perceive has an insubstantial look about it, not misty or ethereal; somehow, a sixth sense kicks in and you just know you are seeing a spirit being.

Of course, when you see a ghostly figure dressed in clothing of a different era, this quickly tells you that you aren't actually witnessing a fancy dress party, but that something completely different is occurring.

In my opinion, there is definitely nothing to fear from a ghost. After all, they cannot hurt you, except perhaps emotionally, making you fearful and frightened.

The majority of older children that I know who have seen a ghost have run screaming into their parents' bedrooms, shivering and shaking with fear - a perfectly natural reaction. However, in my research I have often read that youngsters see ghosts far more often than older people. The reasons quoted for this make sense; young children don't have as many worries and concerns as their older siblings and parents do. They have more time to look around and soak up the atmosphere of their surroundings. Youngsters are far more able to tune into the psychic world and see ghosts.

I remember one day when one of my grandsons was about nine months old. he was sitting on his own on the lawn in the garden of his home. He was unaware that I was watching him through the window. As I watched, he suddenly seemed to spot someone and began chatting away to this invisible person, laughing and waving his arms about. His baby talk and laughter became louder as his excitement grew. Try as I might, I couldn't see who he was talking to. Even the family dog ran into the house, as if he sensed something unreal was taking place.

It was a pity I couldn't ask my grandson who he had been chatting to that summer afternoon, but he was far too young. All I could tell was that he was really enjoying the chat.

He hasn't grown up to have any psychic powers, but he does have a great interest in psychic phenomena, and we've had many an interesting discussion about ghosts and other aspects of this intriguing science.

In this book, I have written about the things that I, and the people I know and trust, have tried and believe in.

Jenny Cockell's book *Yesterday's Children* details how she dreamt of a past life. The book describes her search for her family. Through her dreams and memories, and with the help of local maps and women's groups, she finally tracks them down.

All in all, I was convinced that Jenny Cockell did experience reincarnation as it doesn't seem possible that she could have imagined the whole scenario.

In fact, her book made me even more determined to try and discover more about this most intriguing subject.

One day I was researching regression on the Internet and came across a site that offered books and CDs on self-regression. Here was the opportunity I had been waiting for. I ordered Jenny's book and CD straightaway. I have written further on in this book what happened when I investigated the subject.

A number of years ago, I went to a hypnotherapist

for treatment for a problem I was having. It was a really uncomfortable incident, as I drifted back to my early childhood. I had been assured it would be a pleasant experience, but it was far from that. On regressing, I saw a group of men surrounding a coffin and remember feeling terribly upset. I wanted the sitting to end, but I hadn't been given any key words beforehand should I need them to end the session. I did discover afterwards that the therapist wasn't qualified.

Of course, that was my fault for not checking the register of hypnotherapists before going - a point well worth considering should you ever decide to visit a hypnotherapist.

I do remember years ago being enthralled by a hypnotherapist called Joe Keeton, who was an authority on regression. He undertook thousands of regressions, but never proved conclusively that anyone had led a past life.

Lots of children have imaginary friends. These are, of course, different to ghosts as they are simply figments of a child's imagination. A child can call on their imaginary friend at any time, day or night – they are always there for them – whereas ghosts don't appear to order. We cannot summon them; they appear when they choose. Imaginary friends can be called at will and instantly disposed of!

The imaginary friend is usually called upon by a lonely child, perhaps a child whose older sibling has started school, and they have been left behind. After always having company all day, every day, since the day they were born, they are suddenly alone with many empty hours to fill. No wonder they seek a new friend, and what could be easier than for a child with a fertile imagination to choose an imaginary friend. The friend can be of any age or gender the child chooses, they can look how the child wants them to appear, wear the clothing of their choice and even do the child's bidding. What could be better? No arguments, a biddable friend who will do exactly as asked, play any game, share any storybook, or watch any TV programme the child chooses; in fact, the perfect friend. A friend who can be blamed for any misdemeanour the child has committed.

ANGEL CARDS

These cards have increased in popularity in recent years, and I feel it is because they are easy to read.

I think they are a good starting point for anyone interested in reading the tarot or playing cards.

The cards I have are extremely well presented.

On the box, it says: 'Daily Guidance from Your Angels. Oracle Cards, A 44-Card Deck and Guidebook'. Doreen Virtue is the author of the cards, and also many books.

The cards come with a book of instructions on how you set about your daily readings.

Each card has a beautiful picture covering about fifty percent of it. The meaning of the card is described at the bottom of the card.

Doreen gives a good explanation at the beginning of

the booklet as to how to cleanse the cards and how to give yourself a daily reading.

The cards bring a good feeling when you hold them, and if you're looking for good inspirational advice to start your day, these seem to be one way to go.

As a first step into the psychic world, these cards are excellent.

I also recommend reading *An Angel Called My Name* by Theresa Cheung.

ANIMALS

I think it has been known for centuries that animals have developed strong instincts.

The majority of the dogs I have owned have been extremely sensitive. Coming from wolves, they are bound to carry the genes of the wild, and more often than not, they still use them.

Many dogs sense danger before we humans are even aware of a bad situation.

One of the dogs I owned, a German Shepherd called Connie, was extremely intuitive in certain situations. There was one particular place on our regular walk that she refused to walk past, and I always had to cross the road. I did some research on the area, but I as far as I could find, it had always been fields. There had never been a murder or anything disastrous happening in the locality, so I have always been at a loss as to why Connie reacted the way she did.

It is claimed that some cats are extra-perceptive and

also sense changes in the weather and possible danger well before humans do.

Most animals can sense earthquakes before they occur; they certainly do not need instruments or anything to give them warnings.

I remember a particularly strong earthquake in our area a few years ago. The following morning there were no bird sounds for many hours afterwards; I didn't hear a dog bark all day. Now that is very unusual to say the least.

I've heard that horses sense danger, and along with cats and dogs, they know when their owner is ill.

I've heard of dogs and cats detecting cancer in their owners before the owners are aware of it. In fact, they have saved their owners' lives by being so sensitive. I understand certain breeds of dogs are being trained to do this.

I think it pays to watch our pets as they are able to see and hear far more than we can.

ASTRAL TRAVEL

I had a friend who mentioned he could travel astrally. He told me that after he and his wife had divorced, he was rarely allowed to see his daughter. One night, he decided that he would see if he could travel astrally to see her and ensure she was all right.

He found himself in his daughter's bedroom; he saw that it was painted blue. He also looked at the furnishings and bed coverings.

He told me that when he finally did manage to see his

daughter, he asked her to describe her bedroom and everything she told him confirmed what he had seen. After that, whenever he felt the need to check on his daughter, he used this method.

I have never met anyone else who has done this.

An interesting website to visit is www.thiaoouba.com/astr.htm

ASTROLOGY

I find astrology extremely interesting as it covers such a diverse range. I've never studied the subject in any great depth. Plotting birth charts never appealed to me. What I do enjoy along with thousands of other people is reading my horoscope. I also like reading the various things attributed to the different birth signs such as what colour is related to each star sign. Precious and semi-precious stones are also linked to your star sign, along with flowers and herbs. In fact, it would seem there are any number of different things that make up any particular star sign.

Each star sign has a set of interpretations as to a person's personality traits, their emotional makeup, and even their physical characteristics. The star signs even give a run down on the type of health problems each person might expect to suffer from. The type of work they are best suited to is also given. In fact, from reading a professional astrology book, it would seem your life is pretty well mapped out for you by astrology. Some astrology books I have read even tell you your spiritual home. I have listed the star signs below.

STAR SIGNS

Aries
Mar 21-Apr 20

This person likes to be first in everything. They are always up for a challenge, and are full of energy. A wicked sense of humour leads them to be very popular.

Taurus
Apr 21-May 21

Friendly, generous, well-liked. The person with this sign is always popular and has lots of friends. They are very strong-willed and like to lead.

Gemini
May 22-Jun 21

Gemini people are extremely talkative. They are curious, sociable, and affable. Gemini folk are highly inquisitive and enjoy a new challenge. They do not like commitment.

Cancer
Jun 22- Jul 23

Warm-hearted, generous, and emotional. Cancerians enjoy helping people. They are sensitive to situations and pick up any sign of tension immediately.

Leo
Jul 24- Aug 23

People with this sign are happy, outgoing, and

sociable. There's nothing more that they like than a good old chat. Excellent communicators; they would feel really at home working in the media.

Virgo
Aug 24-Sep 23
Reliable, trustworthy; this sign is also a bit of a perfectionist. Never hasty, they will take their time in making decisions. Virgos are dependable, likeable people.

Libra
Sep 24-Oct 23
Loving, pleasant, and enthusiastic; the person who has this sign is always helpful. Libra is the sign of the scales and are at their best when the balance is right.

Scorpio
Oct 24-Nov 22
Sociable, intelligent, and gracious; it is a pleasure to keep company with Scorpios. They make excellent friends. The person with this sign will give their all to whatever they undertake.

Sagittarius
Nov 23-Dec 21
Kind and supportive, Sagittarians enjoy travel and the company of their families. They are positive, honest, and truthful people. People with this sign like to teach.

Capricorn
Dec 22-Jan 20

Patient, always supportive of others; people with this sign love to help their fellow man. They are realistic people who can be rather outspoken. They are strong-willed.

Aquarius
Jan 21-Feb 18

They are intelligent, welcoming, sociable people who enjoy their independence. They have strong personalities and people feel drawn to them at social gatherings.

Pisces
Feb 19 Mar 20

Pisces people make wonderful friends with their caring and sharing natures. They are tactful and dependable. People with this sign are excellent listeners.

AURA

Some people can see a person's aura - a halo of coloured light that surrounds a person - and can tell from interpreting the colours what has happened in the person's life, what is happening at the present time, and what is going to happen in their future. Each colour that shows in an aura has a different meaning, for example, gold represents healing, green envy, red danger.

Visit www.thisoouba.com/seeau.htm

I was once in a doctor's surgery and saw the doctor's

aura. I was astonished to see small gold lights twinkling around him. I was later informed that these lights appear around a person who has healing powers. That made sense. That was the only time I ever saw an aura around a person. I did once see a glow around some flowers and trees in the garden. It was an amazing sight. At first, I thought there was something wrong with my eyes and went to the optician's. My eyes were fine. I later learnt that everything has an aura.

A person who can see an aura definitely has psychic powers.

AUTOMATIC WRITING

There is a tool that you can buy that is supposed to aid you in this psychic art, though I've never used it. I have practised automatic writing, but it's never grabbed me. Perhaps this is why it never worked for me, but it doesn't mean it won't work for other people. I have spoken to people who use this method successfully on a regular basis.

You are supposed to sit quietly while relaxed, with a pen and pad in hand, empty your mind, and place your writing tool onto the paper. After a few seconds or minutes, the pen will start writing.

This is a good introduction to the psychic journey.

BOOKS

The first book I ever bought relating to tarot cards proved to be the best. Nearly 25 years later, I still have it.

The title is *The Tarot Workshop* by Emily Peach. It contains everything you need to know regarding tarot cards. In my opinion, it outshines any other book relating to the tarot.

There are books in local bookshops and online that cover every aspect of the paranormal: from tarot cards to regression, from time travel to mediums, you name it, you will find it in bookshops.

There has been an explosion of interest in the psychic sciences in recent years and it is now far easier with the Internet to find out about the subject you are interested in. Amazon.co.uk and other online bookshops sell almost any paranormal book that has been published in recent years.

Fiction books that mention ghostly happenings normally have a ring of truth about them. The author has probably experienced some paranormal experience that sparked an idea for the novel.

There are numerous book websites devoted to ghosts, spirituality, astral travel, almost any subject you wish to investigate. Every book you read about the paranormal will help you make the decision of which path you wish to take.

CLAIRVOYANTS

According to Collins Dictionary, a clairvoyant is someone who can perceive someone or something beyond the normal range of senses.

Has a clairvoyant or medium ever changed your life?

I asked myself that question a few weeks ago.

I had been thinking about Diana Princess of Wales, who visited many clairvoyants and mediums in her time. Obviously, she was a very troubled lady and needed constant reassurance that her life was going to improve.

Not finding anyone within her circle who could give her the answers, she turned to alternative therapists in her search for happiness. Apparently, she derived a great deal of comfort from visiting these people, but unfortunately, they couldn't stop what eventually happened to her.

A clairvoyant changed my life with her reading. It intrigued me so much that I bought my first set of tarot cards shortly afterwards.

The reading took place over twenty years ago, not far from where I live. The lady clairvoyant had an office in an empty shop. One day my daughter came to visit me and asked if I would like to go for a reading. I didn't realise that the reading would change the course of my life.

The reader was middle-aged, plump; quite a motherly person. After shuffling the tarot cards, she quickly spread them on the table and proceeded to rattle off the reading at a tremendous speed. I had to keep asking her to repeat what she had said. Fortunately, my daughter stayed in the room with me, and when we were at home she told me what she remembered of the reading. The following day, something the reader predicted came true. I was astonished. Over the following weeks, much of what she had predicted happened.

Discussing it with my daughter one day, I decided I would like to teach myself the tarot cards. I decided there and then to go out and buy some. We caught the bus into Birmingham and I went to W. H. Smiths and purchased a set of tarot cards and a book of instructions. I explain how I taught myself to read them further on in this book.

Mediums and clairvoyants are the 'wise people' of bygone ages, a bit like today's social workers and probation officers, people who help others on a professional basis where family and friends are too close to the equation.

COINCIDENCES

Nearly everyone has heard themselves saying at one time or another, 'Oh, that's a coincidence.'

Some people might say it's more than a coincidence, and it was meant to happen. Say, for instance, when you're thinking of someone and the telephone rings, and it is the person who you were thinking about. Your immediate response is, 'What a coincidence. I was just thinking about you.' Or you start thinking about someone you've not seen in years, and suddenly you bump into them that very day. Again, a coincidence, or is it caused by the paranormal?

COLOURS

Some clairvoyants do what is called 'cold readings' when a client arrives. This immediately brings colour therapy into play and gives a good illustration of a cold reading.

Obviously, in 99% of cases if a client arrives dressed

all in black or very dark colours, the clairvoyant will get the impression that their client is depressed and experiencing a bad time. This isn't always the case as some people simply prefer to wear dark clothing all the time.

Muted colours will tell a clairvoyant that their client is not an outgoing person. Again, not always true. The client could simply be wearing colours that suit their colouring rather than their personality.

If the client is wearing bright, loud clothing that says, 'Hey, look at me,' some clairvoyants will immediately assume that the client is a happy, outgoing person who wants or demands to be noticed. In the majority of cases this is true, but on the other hand, the client could be making a statement. They could be feeling the opposite to how they present themselves and are trying to hide the fact that they are extremely depressed. A professional clairvoyant will be able to spot the depressed client in spite of what they are wearing.

CRYSTAL BALL

The crystal ball is an interesting tool to predict the future. It's also a less frightening way than the tarot cards and playing cards, for example. Some susceptible people take fright on seeing certain cards in the tarot and playing card decks. In fact, on seeing the Death Card in the tarot and the Ace of Spades in the playing cards, most people take fright. When people don't understand the meaning of the cards, the appearance of them can be initially disturbing.

The crystal is an empty vessel, and I find it a magical experience looking into its depths and seeing images appear; it seems like a miracle to me.

The following is a story that I think illustrates the crystal ball perfectly.

I remember about ten years ago whilst visiting my mother at Tewkesbury, she asked me to look in the crystal ball for her. On looking, I was disturbed to see that she and my father would be involved at the scene of an accident. I knew that it wouldn't be serious; I saw that an elderly lady would sustain a small injury and need to be taken to hospital. The lady in question would have a lot of white hair. There was no way I was going to pass this message on to my mother and worry her. I passed the crystal ball back to her, saying that I couldn't see anything. She looked into the crystal herself and immediately said that she could see an elderly lady with a lot of white hair. Mother also said that she could see a lorry, a police car, and an ambulance. It was raining at the scene.

To say I was amazed was an understatement, and I wondered how many other clairvoyants have had this happen to them.

Three days later, my mother rang to say that on the previous evening, she and my father had been travelling towards Redditch, Worcs, when the car in front of them hit a lorry; it was raining at the time. The car driver was an elderly lady with a mass of white hair. She was taken to a hospital, but not detained. This was, of course, a case of precognition; I can only assume we were shown this happening to assure us nothing untoward would happen to my parents.

Reading the Crystal

The way I interpret the crystal is quite straightforward. I pass the crystal to the person I am reading it for, they hold the crystal in both hands for a few minutes, and then return it to me. I then look into it and read the images that are shown to me. On occasions, nothing is shown to me; I am always honest and tell the person concerned that it doesn't mean anything awful is going to happen to them. I advise them to go to another reader or return to me in a month or so.

Someone new to the psychic world would find the crystal ball an excellent starting point to help them develop their skills.

CRYSTALS

There are hundreds of different crystals, far too many for me to include in this book. I will include just a few of my favourites.

Crystals are used by spiritual healers and clairvoyants as an aid in their psychic work.

As with any psychic path, if you are attracted to it and decide to take it up, make certain you fully research the subject and spend as much time as you can practicing it before going public. It is up to you to gain as much knowledge as you can.

Amethyst has healing properties. I had a friend once who found she was turning to alcohol more and more, to help her get through the day. She told me that when she acquired a beautiful amethyst, she carried it with her everywhere and never touched another drop of alcohol.

Snowflake Obsidian - I fell in love with this stone the first time I saw it. I didn't buy it for any other reason apart from feeling attracted to it - always the best reason for buying semiprecious stones.

Quartz - Wonderful mystical quartz, reputed to have healing powers.

Citrine - Golden quartz, promotes positive feeling.

Amber - Because my mom always loved it and it reminds me of her and my sister, it is their birthstone.

Crystals are said to bring an air of calm if placed around the home.

DÉJÀ VU

Feeling as if you have been somewhere before.

Travelling to Wales most weekends with my husband during the 1970s, we would go past a place called Richard's Castle. I was always drawn to this place and felt as if I knew it. One day I mentioned it to my mother and she gasped, saying, 'When you were tiny, I would walk you and Pauline (my sister) up the hill every single day.' No wonder I felt so drawn to it. She never told me why we were in that area and would never talk about it again.

DOMINOES

I used the dominoes when I first trod the psychic path. I can't remember when I first heard that they were a means of divining the future. It could be that I read about them in a library book and felt intrigued enough to try the idea out.

I bought myself a set of dominoes, and a book of instructions, and practised for quite a while, giving myself short readings, and then progressing onto the longer ones. I found them intriguing to say the least, and had quite a bit of success with them. They did leave me wanting to know more and I soon moved onto other ways of divination, searching for the one that was right for me.

The domino symbols have been printed on cards according to this website. www.pagat.com

This website has an interesting history of domino divination: www.mysticboard.com

GHOSTS

Ghosts, some people will tell you, are figments of the imagination. They say there are no such things as ghosts. Where does that leave all the people who have experienced the paranormal? Does that mean that the thousands who say they have seen a ghost have simply imagined it? I don't think so.

Having seen ghosts on many occasions, I know for certain they exist. I wrote earlier that I saw my first ghost when I was a child. Over the years, I have seen many more.

One night I was in bed, settling down to sleep, when a slight noise disturbed me. I opened my eyes and saw my husband's grandmother standing beside my bed. This was unbelievable as Grandma Palmer had been dead many years. The strange thing was she was wearing a royal blue button-up-to-the neck cardigan and a grey pleated skirt, nothing unusual about that, but on her head she was wearing a very large panama sun hat. This was strange indeed as I'd never seen Grandma Palmer wearing a hat except at my wedding.

The next time I saw my mom-in-law, I mentioned seeing Granny Palmer and after describing her clothing and the hat, she fetched me a photograph. It was identical to how I had described her. I was amazed. The photograph had been taken at a cottage that John's parents owned in Wales. Grandma Palmer was sitting outside the cottage enjoying herself.

The only explanation I could think of for seeing John's grandmother was that it was a sign that there are indeed ghosts.

GHOST INVESTIGATING

I am always puzzled as to why some ghost investigators go ghost hunting in vaults, cellars, or tunnels at night. Why would they think a spirit is going to haunt these places? I firmly believe that if you are going to see a ghost, you will, and it won't happen in a dark, damp place underground. Ghosts, in my opinion, can be seen any time of day or night, anywhere. My belief is that a ghost will return to a place where it has been happy in its Earthly life. I believe that if a ghostly sighting is spotted at an accident site, it is simply an impression of what happened and is not actually a ghost.

Ghost investigating is the 'in thing' now and there are a plethora of groups all vying to be the first to investigate a new site.

The majority of the groups have electrical equipment with them to detect any spirits that might be about. Among the items that they take with them are a notepad and pen to record times and measurements from the equipment, torch, digital cameras, infra-red camcorders, tape recorders, voice recognition equipment (electronic voice phenomena) etc. and any other equipment that they feel might be helpful in their quest. Among the group, there is normally a medium who will be able to converse with any ghost that might be found.

Normally what happens is that the group don't hear the ghostly voices until they check their equipment after the event. They are also fortunate in some cases to see ghosts or something unusual on the photographs they have taken.

I have heard it said that if a ghost is present, the temperature drops dramatically and group members immediately sense the chill. Also the thermometer registers this.

'Why would these spirits be hanging around?' I asked one member of a ghost investigation team.

'Maybe because the spirit passed suddenly and has been unable to move on,' they replied. I thought this was a reasonable explanation. There are thousands of unexpected deaths and this could lead to thousands of ghosts/souls being unable to pass to the other side.

The first thing you must do if you are going out as a ghost investigator is ask permission to investigate the site and agree on a time and date, unless you have been invited to investigate the location. Always wear suitable warm clothing and waterproof footwear. A really good point that I have heard mentioned and read about is if you are on any form of medication, take it with you.

By going out as a ghost investigator, you will be on the road to developing your psychic skills. It will make you more observant and more aware of anything to do with the paranormal. On the plus side, you will be meeting people with the same interests who will give you good advice.

NICK DUFFY ON GHOSTS

'Believing in ghosts'... I have to admit that, these days, I'm bordering between complete disbelief in such things and only the vaguest possibility that they might exist. I cannot deny that people believe that they are having such experiences, but I don't really think that the bulk of these things have anything to do with anything truly 'ghostly'. I do believe that personal psychology - or perhaps an isolated quirk or effect of the mind, hypnologic state, micro-sleep, or whatever - accounts for a lot of these encounters to a considerable degree. Unfortunately, especially these days, the belief systems of a lot of people seem to sway their experiences and something rather mundane - noises in the home, the odd object being misplaced, etc - are put down to paranormal effects, when they're not. There is, of course, the possibility that true ghostly events do occur.

I certainly *don't* believe in the spiritual existence of souls, or whatever people want to call them, after death. I most certainly don't think that the dead return after they die. If there is anything to ghosts, I think we're talking about a memory or photograph, rather than anything with an intelligence behind it. Anything that shows an intelligence of some sort - movement of objects and so on - I believe is non-human in nature...

Nick Duffy has been investigating ghosts for over twenty years.

HAUNTED OLD CHANCEL

Not far from where I live is a church building known as The Old Chancel. It was originally the parish church, but as the population increased, a larger church had to be built. The newer church is across the road from the Chancel.

Personally I prefer the Old Chancel building to the new church. It is far more beautiful and has a wonderful atmosphere. I have often sat in the grounds imagining the thousands of people who have walked through there over the centuries.

One day while sitting in the grounds, I heard a sound behind me. On looking round, I saw a man hurrying across the grass heading in the direction of the school that stands to the side of the Chancel. He was dressed in old-fashioned attire and a black gown. At first I thought he was the local vicar, as the vicarage isn't far from the Chancel, but I quickly realised he wasn't. The figure disappeared in front of my eyes.

Subsequently, I discovered that the school had once been the old grammar school. Someone mentioned to me at a later date that the description I gave them of the man fitted his old tutor who had worked at the school many years previously. The tutor had died at least thirty years ago.

Is this further proof of the existence of ghosts, or simply my imagination? I know I saw the figure of the man, so there is no doubt whatsoever in my mind that ghosts exist.

KATHY – A FRIEND'S THOUGHTS ON GHOSTS

Some years ago, when I slept in a different bedroom, I was lying in bed reading when I became aware of the duvet being pulled down. I gingerly looked over the top of my book and actually saw it moving. If I had told my husband, he would never have slept in the room again. This happened on numerous occasions. I never felt frightened or worried by it - just curious. One night, as I was drifting off to sleep, I felt the bed dip and thought, *Oh, that's Alan getting into bed.* I opened my eyes to look and no one was there. I visited my local spiritualist church and received a message that I had a family with me consisting of a mom and dad and seven children. It was the children who were playing with the bedclothes.

Kathy goes on to say…

Ghosts, I believe, are projected by our own minds. I believe that some people pick up on, or sense spirit, and there is something which goes on in our brains allowing us to project an apparition.

My overall personal belief is that I believe in the survival of the personality. We are all made up of cells, energy, and energy can't be destroyed; it can only change into something else. Everyone who enters this world leaves a unique signature on everything they touch, and that remains. I believe that sensitive people can tune into this.

KEN'S STORY

Ken was cycling to work early one misty morning. As he approached Wheatman's Bridge, a motorbike swerved in front of him and the rider fell off. Ken hastily jumped off his bike, ready to give aid. He was mystified when he could find no trace of the man or his motorbike. He searched the area as best he could, but to no avail.

Convinced that he hadn't imagined the whole incident, Ken discussed it with many people. He was relieved to hear that a number of people had had similar experiences.

TELEPHONE HAUNTING
LICHFIELD, STAFFS

Jill recalled this unusual experience.

At the time, she wasn't living at her marital home, having recently separated from her husband. One day her elder daughter telephoned to say that her young sister's car had broken down.

Jill then rang her old home hoping to contact her son, who still lived there at that time. She knew that he had gone away for the weekend, but hoped that he had returned early and could go and pick the young girl up.

She was surprised when a woman answered the telephone. She asked if she had the right number and quoted the one she had dialled. The woman confirmed this and also the address. Jill asked if her son was at home. The woman replied that her son had gone away for the weekend. Jill was so startled that she hung up.

After a few moments, Jill re-tried the number. The same person answered. Again, Jill checked the number and address; once again they were confirmed as being correct. Jill then said, 'But you can't live there, that is my home.'

The voice replied, 'Well, you know that.' It then dawned on Jill that she was, in fact, speaking to herself.

I find the above a very intriguing story.

NEXT-DOOR NEIGHBOUR HAUNTING

I had invited my next-door neighbour to a meeting at our local library. He had accepted my offer and told me he would be in Wales for a few days but he assured me that he would be back in time for the meeting.

The night before the meeting, I had retired to bed. As I was settling down to sleep I heard my neighbour, Herbert, returning. I thought, *Good, he'll be coming to the meeting with me.* I heard him walking up stairs and pottering around; he never bothered with carpets in his upstairs rooms so I could hear his every movement when it was quiet. The next morning not long after I got up, two of my other neighbours popped round and told me that Herbert had died when he was away in Wales. I told them, 'No, he hasn't died. I heard him return last night!' They looked quite shocked. Not as shocked as me though. I really thought I had heard him return. Perhaps his spirit returned that night. I don't know. On reflection, it was a very strange experience.

I know I have mentioned that I don't believe you can contact a ghost at will; but there are people who say it can be done. Doris Stokes, who was a well-known medium, said that placing a photograph of a deceased loved one in a room with a red rose beside it would encourage the person to return. Other people say by relaxing and thinking about the person you wish to contact will open the way for them.

Many people think orbs that show on digital photographs are ghosts. I don't for one minute believe that they are. I am firmly convinced that orbs are dust particles. I just cannot accept that a ghost would show itself in such a manner.

IMAGINARY FRIENDS

As I mentioned earlier in the book, young children create imaginary friends from their imagination. In the majority of cases, this is when they are lonely. I have heard of many cases of this and often seen children playing with their imaginary friends.

The friends normally fade away when the child starts school and makes new friends. It can also happen when a child with no siblings is older and they move to a new area, leaving their old acquaintances behind.

Imaginary friends are not harmful in any way whatsoever. I think in certain cases they are a welcome addition to the family, allowing the child to have a friend, thus permitting them to play and not feel so isolated.

A group I used to attend every week would leave a chair empty for one of their members, who had sadly passed away.

This wasn't left because they thought she was a ghost. I took it that they imagined their friend was still with them at the meeting. It was quite touching to see that they still included her in their group.

INTUITION

I vividly recall an unusual occurrence that happened to me a number of years ago. One of my brothers rang to say he was moving to a new house that weekend. I told him we would go and visit him in a couple of weeks, after he had settled in. He gave me the address.

A few weeks later, I was driving my family to my

brother's new house when my husband asked if I had asked for the directions. 'No need,' I replied, 'I know where it is.' My husband was shocked as I drove straight to my brother's new home.

I'll never know how I knew where his house was as I had never been there before. It was quite a distance from his old home and on a new housing estate away from the town.

I just accept that some things are inexplicable.

MATERIALISATION

A few years ago, I used to read the tarot cards for members of the general public.

One day, a woman arrived for a reading. I didn't know her. She was a nice cheerful lady and we hit it off immediately.

The reading was straightforward and as it drew to an end, I happened to glance across to where she was sitting. I was astonished to see a young girl of about ten years of age sitting beside her. In an instant, I knew she was a ghost even though she looked normal. It's hard to describe the difference, but I couldn't see through her. Maybe the best way to describe the youngster is to say she looked insubstantial.

I promptly described the child to the lady, who said straightaway that the girl was her daughter and the description was how she had looked at that age.

Not only was she surprised, so was I.

Another occasion when I saw a child materialise was when I went to see a clairvoyant. This was quite a number of years ago. The clairvoyant lived about ten miles away. I had heard she did interesting readings and managed to get an appointment.

My husband took me and we found the woman, who lived in a cottage along a quiet country lane. We parked outside in the lane. She was quite an elderly woman and she had forgotten I was going for a reading, but she stopped preparing her tea and took me into the small room where she did her 'readings'.

The reading lasted about twenty minutes and we then returned to the lounge where my husband was waiting. The lounge was stuffed full of furnishings, but I was impressed by the beautiful spiral staircase that wound its way up to the first floor. I glanced back at the clairvoyant and saw a young girl dancing happily around her, and then heard the name of Bill being whispered in my ear. I jumped, more than a little surprised at these two happenings.

I described the young girl to the clairvoyant, who laughed and said, 'That's my twin sister. She died when she was eight years old. Other psychics have told me she is always with me.' She went on to say, 'Bill was a man who ran off with a lot of my money.'

Another occurrence of materialisation happened one evening. I was sitting in the lounge of our home, as my son was just leaving the room. He turned towards me and as I looked at him, the most remarkable thing happened. The shape of a young man materialised in front of him. I found myself saying, 'Charlie will be telling you next week that he has found a new job and will be starting work soon.' I added that it would be a very hot day, despite it being near the end of October. 'He will be wearing a new suit and a mac.' I felt really exhausted after this happening and took myself off to bed.

The following week when my son came home for lunch, he told me in a very matter of fact way that he had met Charlie in the town, who told him he been offered a job. Charlie was wearing the clothes I had described and it was, in fact, a very hot day for the time of year.

One windy autumn morning, two men were cycling to work along the Stafford to Milford road.

One of the cyclists suddenly saw an elderly woman jump out in front of him. He immediately braked hard and she shouted at him that he had to stop immediately as it was dangerous for him to proceed. The woman then disappeared.

He was startled beyond belief, as was his colleague. They recognised the lady as having lived at a small cottage not far away. She had died many years before.

They then saw a huge tree fall across the road just ahead of them. If the woman hadn't materialised when she did, they would have both been killed.

Four entirely different materialisations, but each with a different story to tell.

I am convinced that materialisations do occur. Scientists, however, would no doubt tell us differently and wrap it all up in language that is hard to decipher.

I prefer to believe what I saw with my own eyes and the proof was in the telling and acceptance of the stories.

MEDIUMS

Mediums are people who, we are told, speak to the dead. They don't predict the future - though I have known many who do.

They say their job is to contact the spirit world.

Mediums are said to be a channel for the dead. I haven't quite worked out yet exactly how they do this, but I think they all work along similar lines.

I've seen many mediums in the past and can honestly say not one of them came anywhere near to communicating with the spirit world for me.

I'm not saying they cannot communicate with the other side, just that it has never happened for me.

I have visited those that were recommended to me via word of mouth - always supposed to be the best way of doing things. Not one of them ever gave me conclusive proof of life after death.

One medium I went to see claimed he had my mother with him in spirit. Really? In fact, I had been speaking to my mother before going for the reading. He immediately changed his mind saying it was my grandmother he had with him. Extraordinary, my grandmother was still alive at that time. Dear me, he simply got everything wrong that morning.

One medium told me that it was my fault that she couldn't get in touch with the spirit world. Her reason was I was blocking the spirits. I thought that was an unreasonable thing to say, as more than anything I wanted to make contact with the other side.

I had a couple of telephone readings; these were rubbish. It was the normal clatter: I would move house, win the lottery (I wish) or someone I know would win the lottery. Lots of leading questions were asked. I found it all very airy-fairy. No link to the other side was ever made, apart from one of them seeing an elderly woman with me. You can say that about nearly everyone in the world. No names or descriptions were given to me - very disappointing. All in all, I found it a sheer waste of money.

I do know that a good many people have found a lot of comfort from having readings from mediums.

One medium I have known for many years has a wonderful gift for predicting the future.

Many years ago, I went to see her. I was hoping she would be able to contact the spirit world for me. As soon as I sat down, Doreen told me she couldn't make contact with anyone. Although disappointed, I admired her honesty. She then went on to give me a taped reading.

I must admit that I wasn't impressed with the reading, as I couldn't honestly believe that some of the predictions she had made would happen.

How wrong I was proved to be.

Doreen predicted that I would write books, articles, deal with editors, appear on radio shows, and deal with newspaper journalists.

I put the tape away thinking none of it would come true. In fact, nearly all that Doreen told me that day has happened in ways that I would never have envisaged.

Since then I have had other readings from her, all

equally as interesting.

Despite all the mediums I have visited over the years, never once have I been given proof of life after death.

This doesn't mean that many people have not received proof of the afterlife. If you are thinking of developing as a medium, you should contact the Spiritualists Association. It does take many years and a lot of hard work to become a fully-fledged medium.

NUMEROLOGY

Numerology has been used for thousands of years, and the power of numbers is not to be taken lightly. By using numerology, you can open many previously unopened doors in your subconscious.

Here is a simple explanation of how numerology can help you unlock the power of your mind.

By using numbers to help you understand various aspects of your life, you will be using a very ancient craft. Used in conjunction with the alphabet, numbers become very powerful.

Each letter of the alphabet represents a number. I have written a table below:

1	2	3	4	5	6	7	8	9
A	B	C	D	E	F	G	H	I
J	K	L	M	N	O	P	Q	R
S	T	U	V	W	X	Y	Z	

NAMES

You can work out your own personal number by reducing the letters of your name to a number.

For example if your name is Carol, reduce it to numbers, i.e.

C = 3 A = 1 R = 9 O = 6 L = 4 total = 23, 2 + 3 = 5

You can now check out your personal number, or try it on your family or friends' names. This in turn will lead you on to more discoveries using this system.

Number 1

People whose name reduces to number one are normally intelligent, hard-working, industrious people. They have a lot of charisma and can literally charm the birds from the trees when they put their minds to it. The teaching profession appeals to people of this ilk as they have a love of teaching and learning. They have a very helpful nature, but at times they can be a little impatient if the person they are dealing with doesn't immediately grasp what they are being taught.

They always like to be at the very top of the ladder. Perversely, they can at times be quite weak emotionally.

Number 2

People with this number will always put others before themselves. Their serene nature hides their inner conflicts, they are always ready with a smile, their easy-going nature can often leave them with no time for themselves or their families. They can back themselves into a corner by overloading themselves with work for others and leaving themselves in a mess. They find themselves bogged down with too much to do and no time to do it. This can leave them feeling exhausted.

These people like to travel the middle line; they hate to be picked out of a crowd, preferring very much to stay out of the limelight.

Number 3

This number represents the communicator, the talker, highly imaginative, full of good ideas and always ready to lend a helping hand. They readily accept any offers that come their way in life. Number three people have a great love of life and can adapt to any change of circumstances with ease. Don't be fooled by this apparent show of confidence; underneath they are really saying, 'Don't hurt me or I'll crumble.'

They have to beware because they can easily be hoodwinked. Their easy-going nature can sometimes lead them down the wrong path.

Number 4

Any person who has this number will have a shy, retiring nature. They are highly individual people, intelligent and creative. They can turn their hand to almost anything. Full of good ideas, at times they tend to let their imaginations run away with them and find they don't have enough time to complete their given tasks. Home lovers, they like to surround themselves with all their treasures and are more than content to stay at home rather than hit the nightclub scene. These people can easily fall into the trap of being their own worst enemy. By not mixing socially, others can view them as being standoffish and boring.

Number 5

A real go-getter, this number likes to be out in front. Often impatient, they have the need to always be on the go. They are always willing to work, but at times lack the patience to complete the task in hand before moving on to something else. They have a great sense of humour and love being in good company. Number five people are people-persons and you can depend on them to keep a party going.

They are best suited to a job that involves people. People with this number need to stand back from themselves and give other people their own space, i.e. their powerful personality can be rather over-powering at times.

Number 6

A job in the United Nations would suit this number. A number that loves to be loved and enjoys being piggy in the middle to help keep the peace. This sign likes to please and likes people to like them. Nothing is too much trouble for them in their quest to please.

Number six people can do very well in business ventures. At times they can seem to be a bit slipshod, but this is just a front to hide their shrewd business brain.

Number 7

Always diplomatic, people with the number seven value are suited to working in the caring profession. They are kind, compassionate, and understanding. When dealing with others, they will always lend a sympathetic listening ear.

Number seven people always have the will to succeed, but unfortunately they sometimes fall by the wayside because they don't pay attention to smaller details. Warm-hearted, generous to a fault, perhaps a little bit too generous for their own good, they tend to give more than they can really afford, not just materially, but also on the emotional front, leaving themselves drained of energy and finances. Their motto is, 'It is better to give than receive'. They do tend to go a bit over the top at times in their effort to please.

Number 8

The organizer is this number. Their whole life is geared to organization, not just for themselves, but also for other people. They have a love of life and, provided everything runs like clockwork, they are happy. Highly motivated, they make good leaders. The trouble is they expect everyone to meet their own high standards; when they don't, they become very impatient.

People with this number often seem distant but they find they can be easily hurt; they hide their feelings and then, to their detriment, come across as being cold and brusque. Relationships can prove difficult.

Number 9

People with this number are very strong-willed characters; they attract others to them like magnets. They like nothing better than being up and out there in the world. Normally, they will have a great circle of friends and admirers. They are well-blessed, confident people with a strong character. They will never knowingly upset anyone; if by some mischance they do, they will go to the end of the world to put matters right. But beware, people who have the number nine are very volatile and can be tactless.

Number 10

Outgoing, easy to get on with, people with the number ten have a rigid set of principles and don't like to be crossed. Once they make an enemy, beware, because they can be formidable. It is rare for anyone to win an argument with this person. They stick to their guns no matter what. There is never an in-between for these people; black is black and white is white. On the other hand, they make brilliant friends and will never let you down.

Ouija Boards

Ouija boards were quite popular in the 1970s and were sold as a game. I wasn't put off by all the stories that they were nasty evil things that attracted bad spirits. Along with a few friends, we set it up one night and were astounded when the pointer moved on its own accord and began spelling out messages. 'Who's pushing it?' someone asked. Immediately, the people using it quickly made denials and a ghostly silence descended on the room, as the pointer moved faster and faster around the board. It gave out many messages that no one could possibly have known about, and we were all astounded by this mysterious piece of equipment. We wondered how a small plastic pointer could seemingly move on its own volition and point to the letters and numbers printed around the board, spelling out messages. After each message, the room temperature seemed to drop, making the whole affair seem even spookier. The messages carried on coming thick and fast for quite a while, but then their tone seemed to change in content; instead of giving out positive answers to questions, negative ones began to be spelt through and the atmosphere became charged. We all became very worried and packed it away. In fact, I refused to have it in the house and it was thrown in the shed; later when we moved, it went into the dustbin.

Over the years, I have realised that really the board was not a scary object; we ladies just frightened each other. At the end of the day, it was just a printed card with letters and numbers on it. The good predictions that the board made in the early part of the evening did come true. I was really surprised and happy for the people concerned.

I have known a few people who have used Ouija boards with surprising results. My own opinion is that they should only be sold to responsible adults, never youngsters, who are extremely impressionable and can become hysterical at the littlest thing. Fear engenders fear, and young people shouldn't be allowed to buy the boards. There should always be an experienced person in charge of any meeting when a Ouija board is being used.

PALM READING

This is still quite a popular means of foretelling the future. The lines on your hands apparently not only give an insight into your character, but also tell you how your life is going to pan out.

Some palmists can actually tell people who consult with them what their professions are going to be, when they will marry and divorce, or separate if they live together. They can tell you at a glance, from the number of lines on your hand, how many children you will have or miscarry if you wanted to know.

They have been known to predict big wins; at one time it was the football pools - but now it's the National Lottery. The palmist will also tell you if you are going to inherit money. In fact, experienced readers are able to cover nearly every twist and turn your life will take. Not only that, if you return after a few years, they will give you a further reading as obviously the major lines on your hands change and even more happenings begin to show.

I visited a palmist once when I was on holiday in Meols, and was more than shocked when she gave me the initials of my husband's Christian names and also my children's names, simply by looking at the centre of my left hand. I was amazed as I had never met her before.

My husband wasn't shocked at all, 'Why should you be surprised?' he countered. 'After all, you've known my name since we met. You also know our children's names.' Typical man, I thought.

I think palmistry is a really interesting way to develop your skills.

PENDULUM

It's said that using a pendulum can help you gain answers to your questions.

I use an Austrian crystal on a silver chain.

Below is an explanation of how I use the pendulum.

Write the word *yes* and *no* on separate sheets of paper and place them a short distance apart. Hold the pendulum between the sheets of paper. Keep the pendulum as steady as possible. If it is going to activate, it should gradually begin to swing either towards the '*yes*' or the '*no*'. Its speed will gradually increase until it seems to have a life of its own - quite remarkable!

I have used this method numerous times with a significant degree of accuracy.

Of course, it all comes down to free will whether or not you accept the answer the pendulum gives you.

I was advised by someone who used this method never to ask more than three questions at any one time. She also said it was wrong to ask if you were going to come into money.

The technique below is very old, but is still used today.

If you thread a wedding ring onto a length of cotton or wool and hold it over the stomach of a pregnant woman, it will tell you the sex of the child. If it circles around, it will be a girl; if it swings backwards and forwards, it will be a boy. Of course, this superstition pre-dates scans.

PLAYING CARDS

I have used playing cards to predict the future when I haven't had a deck of tarot cards to hand.

I got to know a lady who read playing cards many years ago. She had offices in Birmingham City Centre where she practised her craft. Joanne, the lady reader, was extremely good at her job, and was very professional. I had readings from her on a regular basis. Occasionally, we would swap readings. I would read the tarot for her and she would then give me a reading from the playing cards. It made for quite an interesting couple of hours. In one of the readings I did for her, I saw her receiving an acceptance for a book she had sent to a publisher. I thought, *Nice one, Joanne*, and was delighted for her. The book did really well.

After having a number of readings with Joanne, I went out and bought myself a pack of playing cards and her book, and taught myself the basics of the cards. I found it quite difficult, as I would automatically put the meanings of the tarot to the playing cards. Playing cards are very similar to tarot cards, except from there being 78 cards in the tarot and 52 cards in the playing cards.

The major difference from the tarot cards is that there aren't any pictures on them, apart from the high cards, i.e. King, Queen, Jack, and Ace.

This is an excellent website for a history of the playing cards: www.wopc.co.uk

POSITIVE THINKING

Positive thinking is so important in today's lifestyle.

Having used it in every corner of my life, I know it works. Below, I have written a few of the ways I use positive thinking in my life.

Everyone gets down and out; it's part of life; the ups and downs, the swings and roundabouts. For every down there is an up. But at times, it can seem there are more downs than ups and that's when the negative thinking begins to set in. If we can recognise the signs, then we can immediately work on the positive thinking, before things get out of hand.

Once you slip into negative thinking, then you are on the downward spiral. It's so easy to allow your thoughts to go this way, and you soon begin to get a jaundiced view of the world. By being able to see yourself slipping, you can bring yourself back from the brink.

You can turn a negative into a positive by seeing the good side of someone or something instead of dwelling on the bad. Always try and turn a negative thought into a positive thought and see how much better you feel.

By telling yourself that the glass is half-full rather than half-empty, it immediately turns your thoughts towards being positive.

'Sunshine always follows the rain,' is another old saying that can work wonders.

I know myself that some things are extremely hard to overcome. The death of a much-loved family member or pet is a traumatic event in anyone's life. After the initial shock, anger can begin to set in, followed by regrets. If you remember that everyone experiences these emotions, it can help. Bereavement counselling helps many people. Other people find it is time that helps them to come to terms with the death of a loved one. Never feel guilty at being depressed, unhappy, or sad. Simply accepting that what you are experiencing is an entirely normal happening will help you.

For some people, it can take longer to accept that they won't see their loved one again; others seem to move on faster. There are no hard and fast rules. Looking ahead and knowing that eventually the hurt will ease helps you to come to terms with this eventuality.

I remember an old saying that was around many years ago. It went: 'I can, I shall, I will.' I remember people going around muttering this under their breath as they passed me. It did help a few people to take up a new challenge.

There are many books on the marketplace about positive thinking, and lots of stories about people who have achieved their ambitions and turned their lives around through deploying different methods.

Simply by putting a favourite CD on can work wonders.

I have heard psychologists recommend people watch the Jerry Springer Show! It is funny. The television programme *'Most Haunted'* has the same effect on me! It certainly makes me laugh.

A walk or jogging or running is wonderfully therapeutic, or walking the dog if you have one of course. Getting out of the house even for a short space of time can help you leave your troubles behind. Any form of exercise that suits you can only do you good.

Go on a shopping trip – wonderfully therapeutic if you enjoy shopping.

Meet up with a good friend or a group of friends.

Share your troubles with a trusted friend.

Always give yourself something to look forward to each day and make time for yourself, be it half an hour or an hour. Make it known that it's your time, your space, and that you don't welcome intruders unless it's an emergency of course.

Some people write down what they want on a sheet of paper and pop it under their pillows before they go to sleep. They swear this helps them achieve their aims. A case of whatever helps lift your spirits can only be good for you.

One of the main things is to turn a negative into a positive and make it work for you. Once you have achieved this, you will be able to pass the advice that works for you on to your clients.

PREDICTIONS

A few years ago, I told my family that my sister would have a baby and it would be a girl. I added that the baby would be born in July of the following year.

My daughter's baby was due to be born in July of that year. I told her that she would have a boy and that he would be born in June.

My family thought my predictions were hilarious. In particular, the prediction about my sister had them falling about with laughter, as she was in her thirties and had always said she would never have a child.

I took no notice of them, knowing I was right, though I must admit I began to have some misgivings the more they teased me.

My predications came true. My daughter's son was born at the end of June and my sister's daughter arrived at the beginning of July.

I don't know where the predictions came from that day, as I hadn't been thinking about babies or anything to do with them. The predictions arrived completely out of the blue.

Proof again that psychic phenomenon comes in different guises.

PREMONITIONS

Having had premonitions myself, I did some research on the subject and was surprised at the amount of people who have had premonitions that came true.

The following story concerns a premonition that I had.

Rugeley – Stafford Road, Staffs

During the mid-eighties, I travelled to work along the Rugeley to Stafford road daily. The scenery is really beautiful, as on one side of the road are the woodlands of Cannock Chase and the other is bordered by the grounds of Shugborough Hall, owned at one time by the Earl of Lichfield.

All in all, it made for a really pleasant drive as the scenery is always a joy to see in whatever season. However, one summer's day as I approached the section of road that leads down into Milford Common, I had what I can only describe as a feeling of impending doom. These feelings became so strong over the ensuing days that one morning I decided there was no way I could drive my normal route to work. I took an alternative road across the top of the Chase; it took me longer, but I didn't feel threatened.

A few days later, I heard that there had been a road accident along the Rugeley to Milford road. It had happened around the time I normally went to work. I remember going cold when my employer told me of the accident.

From whom I received my warning I will never know, but I will always be grateful to my guardian angel.

PSYCHOMETRY

This is the art of reading by holding an object belonging to a client.

The person doing the reading asks their client to pass

a small object to them, preferably a watch, bracelet, or necklace. It should be something they have had about their person for a few hours. The reader then holds the object and is able to tell the client something that has happened to them in the past, what is happening in their lives now, or predict something that will happen in the future. Having done this myself, I know it works.

The client must own the object that is used.

I did a psychometry reading for a client a few years ago. As with most readings, I soon forgot about it. Three years later, the lady client returned and told me that I had written down the names of her future in-laws, and described in detail everything to do with her wedding, even down to the flowers of her wedding bouquet. I was obviously very pleased for her.

REIKI

Reiki is a form of healing that can be used at any level, whether spiritual, emotional, or mental, so it is claimed. The person giving the Reiki is said to be simply a channel for the healing.

The healing can be carried out anywhere at any time. The recipient doesn't have to focus on the treatment or do anything in particular whilst it is being channelled.

It is claimed that minor illness can be cured almost immediately, while more serious illnesses take more time. The benefits to the patient are said to be highly beneficial.

REGRESSION

Many hypnotherapists have found that past life regression has helped cure people of phobias and certain illnesses such as asthma and eczema. Obviously they make no promises or claims, but they are able to say that patients have returned saying that since having returned to a previous life under hypnosis, they have come to terms with their fears. Others say that their allergies have disappeared.

I have never been professionally regressed; I have always thought that as I am an avid reader of historical novels and history books, I wouldn't be a good subject.

I have read that many therapists are convinced that the consciousness lives on after death of the physical body. It's all a bit deep for me, I must admit. As with anything to do with the paranormal, it is intriguing because no one knows what happens after we die. We can only surmise.

It would be wonderful to know that we do live on, and in the case of people who have met a terrible end, that they get the chance to return and live a new, happier life.

I self-regressed myself after buying a CD from the Internet. It was pretty straightforward, not a bit scary, and I really felt in control, unlike the occasion when I went for hypnotherapy a number of years ago. On that occasion, I didn't feel in control at all. I found it quite a worrying experience.

The first time I self-regressed, I was quite sceptical but decided to give it a try. Within seconds I found myself in a street in a town known as Smethwick. I have heard of Smethwick, but have never been there. I had no idea what it looks like or what it is known for. When I found myself in Smethwick, it was the 1950s; this was in 2009.

I found myself in quite a long street of houses. There was a coal lorry down the street on the opposite side of the road. In the distance I saw tall factory chimneys. There were girls skipping with a rope. Some other children were larking about. A small plump girl was playing by herself. I noticed a woman wearing a light, fawn-coloured, belted coat walking along the road. She looked terribly upset and she was surrounded by a group of women who were trying to comfort her. I gathered her husband had just died.

I also got the impression of the name Windmill.

This was a very strange occurrence and the following day I tried again. I saw the same people in the same street; it was as if a video camera was on replay.

Doing some research afterwards, I bought a book about Smethwick that contained old photographs of the area. I was surprised to find that there is a Windmill Lane in Smethwick, and I also saw photographs that looked very similar to places I had seen during the regression. I am currently researching the area.

I left it alone for a few months after that, but recently I decided to try again.

I settled down and deployed the instructions. The first thing I saw was very strange indeed. It looked like an enormous wing of an aeroplane. I followed the length of it with my eye and at the end of it I saw bird feathers and dead birds. It was a terrible sight. The scene then changed and I saw people with strange drawings covering their faces, and white marks painted on their nose in squares. There were men wearing headdresses such as Indians wear; it was all very strange. As my eyes took in the scene, I saw some of the native people holding a huge copper pan filled with water. There were a lot of people holding it up high. I thought they were making an offering to the gods. I saw the sky changing colour. It was the brightest sunset I had ever seen; bright oranges and reds. I realised that there was a tremendous fire raging around the people. The noise became horrendous, as did the smoke. Then there was nothing, just peace and darkness. A very strange and disturbing scene.

A JOURNALIST'S STORY

I was fascinated to read in our local newspaper *The Post* of one of the paper's journalists going for regression. The article was very interesting to say the least. The journalist concerned, Theresa Larner, found herself re-living a life in 1882 as a farmer's wife. Her husband was named Jack, and the couple had a two-year-old son. Their home was in Southern Ireland. Theresa was also stepmother to her husband's two older children from an earlier marriage; their mother had died in a fire.

Theresa brilliantly described various happenings in that lifetime, and I envied her experience. I also considered her very brave to go into the unknown and re-live a previous life, not knowing what she would see.

I asked her what it was like and she said she actually felt as if she was living that lifetime; everything was crystal clear. I can only say it sounded astonishing. So did her colleague Michael's regression, who Theresa has since married.

Michael also gave some vivid accounts, names, dates, towns, and descriptions of clothes; it was all very intriguing.

The article certainly gave me plenty of food for thought.

LYN'S THOUGHTS ON REGRESSION

Kathy, (Lyn's sister), and I have had quite a few conversations about this subject, as have my brother and I. Each of us differs in our beliefs. Regression is a grey area for me because I have seen and read accounts of regressions by therapists and psychologists. In many cases, the subject is led by the questions. Also, people's experiences of the world begin as they take their first breath. Their five senses begin to work immediately and they take in sight, sound, taste, smell, and touch. All of these experiences remain in the subconscious. As they progress through life, every single second of their lives is indented on their subconscious. The conscious mind may not remember, but when stimulated, the subconscious has the record.

However, I don't rule out the regression subject completely. I have an open mind.

Kathy tells me that I analyse things too much. That's

true, because how will we ever find the truth if we don't first find the untruths? Again, I don't rule out reincarnation. From the scientific angle we each carry our ancestors' genes, in some ratio, so technically they do sort of reincarnate through us. But as for the reincarnation in previous lives, I need to get my head round that a bit more.

REINCARNATION

The subject of reincarnation always promotes discussion and controversy. It is an extremely deep subject and no one can claim to have the answers. This is what makes it so interesting. Have we lived before? Who knows? Do we return in another body and live another life? I don't think we are anywhere near to finding the answer. Perhaps Kathy, who wrote earlier, hit the nail on the head when she said, 'Our personality lives on.' I think in a way I could accept that.

There again, I sometimes feel we do return and live again. I cannot explain why I think this. Perhaps it's simply that I don't want to think that this is all there is, and instead, I hope that we get offered another chance.

Some religions believe in reincarnation and accept it as fact that we reincarnate. Perhaps we are given the choice? Who knows? I certainly don't. No one has ever proved life after death but then no one has proved the contrary.

RUNES

The runes are a really exceptional aid to clairvoyance. They can help you develop spiritually. This in turn helps to develop your psychic powers.

Just by picking up a book of rune instructions, you are immediately drawn into the ancient practice of rune casting. I am a firm believer in reading the runes. They contain so much information that helps you understand what is going on within you emotionally and spiritually.

I would advise anyone who is thinking of becoming a reader to have a set of runes and use them at least once a week. By following their advice, you will be able to determine how you are developing spiritually.

SPELLS

When the words 'casting a spell' are mentioned, people immediately think of witchcraft and black magic; imaginations go into overdrive thinking of witches dancing around bonfires at midnight, making sacrifices in an effort to gain what they want.

This is a fallacy, of course; a spell is just another way of being positive. In other words, concentrating all your thoughts on what you want to achieve.

Objects are used to create spells, but this is really just another way of helping you concentrate. It is a matter of believing in yourself, knowing what you want, and going all out to get it. If deploying an object helps you to focus, then there is nothing wrong with it.

Love spells are incredibly popular and there is no

harm in using them, as long as the person you want to be with is free, of course.

One love spell has been around for years, and it is very simple. All you need is a photograph of yourself and the person you want to be with. If you have a few strands of the person's hair, all the better. Place the hair, along with a few wisps of your hair, on one of the photographs, then lay the other photograph on top of it. Tie them together with thread and put them in an envelope. Keep the envelope under your pillow or in your bag/wallet. It is important to keep thinking about the photographs throughout the following days. As with any spell, if it's meant to happen, it will. This spell can be repeated every week for a month.

At one time, a couple of dolls were used for this spell but with the advent of photography, the dolls were dispensed with.

Spells are wrong when you wish for bad things to happen to someone. There is an old saying that what you give out you get back threefold, and it's true. If you send out negative thoughts to someone, they will come back to you in unexpected ways, and not always good.

SPIRIT BOARD

The spirit board is very similar to a Ouija board. I purchased one last year to compare it with the Ouija board I had thrown away many years ago.

It is white whereas the original one was black. It has also been laminated. On the whole it has a different feel to it all together. The only trouble with it is that it has no planchette and it categorically states that it needs at least two people to operate it. That leaves me at a huge disadvantage, as I am the only one in my household who has a fascination with the paranormal. Mention Ouija boards or Spirit boards to anyone here and they back away, despite them never reading or trying anything to do with the paranormal.

I just have to try things out and reach my own conclusions.

Deciding not to be beaten, I attempted to use my index fingers. Ridiculous, yes, but I have to try these things. Then I had an inspiration. I would try a pendulum - why not? I had nothing to lose.

Placing the laminated card on my knees, I held the pendulum over the board and steadied it. Remarkably, it started to move immediately. Despite feeling a bit daft, I mentally asked if there was anyone there. It swung wide and fast around the 'yes'.

I then asked if it had a message for me. Again - 'yes'. The pendulum then started to swing towards the alphabet and hovered over the initial P and began to swing rapidly round it. I thought of my sister Pauline, who died 31st December 1996, and the pendulum swung back to the 'yes' and circled at great speed. I was amazed and proceeded to see if I could receive another message.

The pendulum spelt out the word 'the' and also 'cus', but then it ran out of steam.

It was quite puzzling and I put it away and read a

book until retiring to bed.

That night, I dreamt of Pauline. It was a happy dream. When I awoke I felt quite peaceful and calm, not a bit worried by the dream. That was the first time I had dreamt of my sister since she died. I had been trying to make some kind of contact with her since her death.

I have visited Spiritualist churches, mediums, and clairvoyants and not one of them have ever picked up on her, so to dream of her and seeing her happy was so good, particularly as she had led a mostly unhappy life. I don't think the dream was a coincidence. Some would say it was because I had thought of her before going to sleep that night. I would dispute that; I think of her *every* single night without fail before I go to sleep.

Radio 4 plays a few bars of the tune, *'Sailing By'*, every night at 12.45 pm; it's on just before the shipping forecast. I listen to it as it takes me back to my childhood. I get a picture of Pauline and me sitting on a beach at Beesands - a small fishing village in the south of England. It's a late summer evening and we are sitting talking and laughing. The sea is lapping at our feet and you can hear and smell the fishing boats unloading their catch. It was one of those magical childhood times that stay with you forever.

So I can say with all honesty that I feel the board did bring Pauline to me that night.

The following night, I had the most frightening nightmares ever. Could the nightmares be related to my using the board? I don't know. Perhaps it was a coincidence, not that I had been reading or watching anything remotely violent as I dislike that type of entertainment. On reflection, I have had many nightmares over the years so I can't honestly say it was the Spirit board that was to blame.

TAROT CARDS

In a word, yes, I believe in tarot cards. I am convinced that they give you an insight into the future. If you have a reading from a professional reader, they should be able to tell you what lies in your immediate future and what lies ahead for the next twelve months. If you are experiencing trouble, a professional reader will be able to tell you when your life will begin to improve.

Of course, it depends on what you are looking for from the sitting. You may well just be looking for a general reading and the person giving the reading will be able to give you an insight into the year ahead.

Obviously, every tarot card reader reads the cards differently.

Having had many readings from different people over the years, I have reached the conclusion that the one reading that came more or less true as the reader had predicted was given to me by a gypsy lady who I visited at Aberystwyth. She had premises on the pier.

The first reading I had with her was in the early summer a number of years ago. It was only a short reading. In fact, when I popped in for the reading I had very little money on me and the woman offered a longer reading or for a cheaper fee, a shorter reading. Due to lack of ready money at that time, I had to opt for the shorter reading. She predicted quite a few things that came true over the following months. Later on in the summer, I *just* happened to find myself in Aberystwyth again and I decided to have the longer reading this time.

This reading proved to be interesting, if not very promising, and I pushed the predictions she gave me to the back of my mind.

Later the following year, I had good reason to remember the woman's words when my handbag was robbed in Birmingham city centre late one afternoon. It was one prediction that I definitely didn't want to come true.

Some might say, 'Well, if it's going to happen, it will.' I agree, and do we want to know if we're going to be robbed? Well, no, but I couldn't control the words that came out of her mouth. She read what was in the cards and I never expected her to tell me that. Other incidents she mentioned did happen, and despite her telling me bad news, I couldn't fault her.

I taught myself to read the tarot cards, and for a few years, I gave readings to the general public and also read the cards for myself.

I find them an excellent guide to see what's coming up in the near future, and also over the following twelve months.

I built up a clientele, who visited me on a regular basis and still keep in touch with me to this day, despite my giving up the card readings a long time ago.

I also taught myself other ways of using the tarot

cards, how to make your wishes come true, and how to get answers to your questions.

I have visited many tarot card readers over the years. I always think it's interesting to see how other people work. Some of what I have been told has come true, but I must admit, unless it's written down or taped, I often forget when a lot of information is fired at me in a short space of time.

When I acquired my first set of tarot cards, I quickly became hooked. The more I used them, the more I wanted to know. Every spare minute I had would be spent teaching myself how to read them.

I would give myself readings and when I was certain I had a good grasp of the subject, I began doing short readings for my family and friends. All in all, it took me a long time before I felt sufficiently confident to put myself in the public eye.

I decided I would only use the cards to help people, thus ensuring they would always be true for me and whoever I was reading for. I also determined I would only do four readings a week. My thinking on this was that if I used the cards too much, they would become tired.

I must admit that tarot cards fascinate me even after twenty years; I still wonder how a set of picture cards can predict the future.

Gypsies say that you shouldn't read the cards for yourself. But then how are you going to teach yourself to read the cards unless you practice reading for yourself?

You are the perfect person to judge your readings in my opinion. How else are you going to know if what you predict happens?

By reading for yourself, you can't go wrong, and you get a free reading.

READING THE TAROT CARDS

Today there are numerous decks of cards to choose from - many are modern day designs. I favour the more traditional tarot designs, but as usual, it comes down to personal choice. What feels right for you will work better for you.

There are 78 cards in a pack of tarot cards. There is a major arcana and a minor arcana. Some people prefer to do readings just from the major arcana, saying that this set takes precedence over the minor deck. I prefer to use both sets, shuffled together, to give a good general mix of what lies ahead.

The one golden rule of tarot is never let anyone borrow your cards. You are the only person who should give readings from them. It is bad practice to allow other people to use your cards.

Obviously if you are giving a client a reading, they have to shuffle the deck. They should then immediately pass it back to you, then afterwards, you should shuffle the cards well to remove the client's reading. Before giving another reading, the cards should once again be shuffled. Any negative thoughts and impressions will then be removed.

Use a small piece of black silk to wrap the cards when they are not in use.

There are many different spreads that are used for giving readings. It is entirely up to the student which one they choose. As with selecting a deck of cards, the spread that they are most attracted to is the correct one for them.

Once things start happening, your confidence increases and you can then move on to more complex readings.

Over the years, I have put my own interpretations to the cards.

Take the card called *The Fool* in the tarot deck. To me, this card has come to represent expense rather than the traditional meaning.

The cards of *news* normally mean telephone calls and the cards that they are pointing to tells you what the person calling is going to tell you.

If the *Magician* card appears in a straightforward reading, the simple interpretation is doing something personal for yourself, i.e. combing your hair, cleaning your teeth, polishing your shoes. But as with all the cards, it depends where it falls in the reading. It is a matter of practicing readings constantly until the cards speak to you.

When I started to teach myself the tarot, I commenced by learning the major arcana, then continued on to the minor arcana. I have listed my own meanings to the tarot below.

THE MAJOR ARCANA

The deck contains 22 cards and are the most important in the tarot deck. They override the remaining 56 cards of the minor arcana.

The Fool

This card represents an expensive time ahead of you.

Reversed

This shows you will be over-spending in a big way and should make you aware of your upcoming actions.

The Magician

When this card appears in a reading, its simple meaning is that something happens whilst you are doing something for yourself.

Reversed

A lot of indecision regarding a project will surround you.

The High Priestess

This card shows that you will be speaking to a woman who has a lot of influence in something that you have a great interest in. Most likely this will be to do with the paranormal.

Reversed

Don't trust advice that will be given to you.

The Empress

Dealing with a young lady of child-bearing age.

Reversed

A young woman having fertility problems.

The Emperor

A knowledgeable older man; he is not a member of any professional body or has any training, apart from life that is. He is someone who can be trusted, and should be listened to.

Reversed

Do not trust this person at all.

The Hierophant

A lady who will give you good advice and will listen and guide you when you seek help from her. Normally this person is an older woman.

Reversed

A person who causes trouble and can be very spiteful. This is often due to jealousy.

The Lovers

Not as normally shown on the television or in films, as a couple of lovers getting together. Usually in a reading, this card simply means making decisions around your personal life. Making wise choices.

Reversed

Ill-conceived ideas around a relationship. When you see this in a reading, take heed of the warning.

The Chariot

An alteration in your plans.

Reversed

Disharmony, a feeling that everything has got out of control. A need to take action fast.

Strength

Seeking emotional help from someone you know who has a lot of self-control in all matters relating to emotional needs.

Reversed

Giving in too easily. Being weak and acting defenceless. Acting impulsively.

The Hermit

Taking professional advice. This does not necessarily mean a consultant or a doctor to do with medical matters. It could be a solicitor, optician, dentist, or even a librarian. Do not panic when you see this card.

Reversed

You could well be acting lazily or out of character by being stubborn and refusing help that is offered.

The Wheel of Fortune

This card shows (depending on other cards surrounding it) that life goes on despite changes.

Reversed

Trying to resist changes that are offered.

Justice

Feeling as if you have been badly treated. Standing up for

yourself and not letting others put on you.

Reversed

Complications with something that has been troubling you.

The Hanged Man

A change of circumstances or simply making decisions about your lifestyle.

Reversed

A lot of indecision surrounding you can lead to upset within your domestic and emotional life.

Death

This is the card that frightens people when they have no understanding of its true meaning. The card represents a rebirth of the self; it could be a whole new way of life or simply a new beginning. Much depends on the cards surrounding it.

Reversed

A reluctance to change anything within your lifestyle. Fear of new beginnings. Tiredness, possibly depression.

Temperance

An understanding of many situations, being able to see the core of the matter and being diplomatic.

Reversed

Getting angry for no good reason. Poor judgement.

The Devil

Not a bad card by any means. An unexpected slight mishap will occur.

Reversed

Being overbearing and trying to take over situations that are not of any concern to you.

The Sun

Means exactly that: great happiness.

Reversed

Life falls apart for a time.

The World

Happiness will surround you due to an unexpected happening.

Reversed

Things will take longer than you think to reach a conclusion.

Of course, with all the foregoing cards, the outcome depends on what comes before and after the card.

The only thing I have found wrong with the tarot is that when it comes to describing people, it isn't very accurate. I have explained this to people who have had readings from me, and I have told them that I have used my clairvoyant skills to describe people. Obviously, the tarot is only a guide and once you start doing readings, clairvoyance comes into play.

THE MINOR ARCANA

THE SUIT OF SWORDS

This suit of cards generally represents powerful and swift-moving action. It is a suit to watch closely; take particular note of when and where one of its cards appear in a spread.

Ace of Swords

Going somewhere you have never been before.

Reversed

Plans disrupted, life becomes unbearable for a short time.

The King of Swords

A powerful and forceful man.

Reversed

A scheming, ruthless man.

The Queen of Swords

A woman who goes all out to get what she wants.

Reversed

A spiteful, devious, untrustworthy woman.

The Knight of Swords

The card of important news.

Reversed

A person who goes all out to disrupt people's lives.

The Page of Swords

Hearing the day-to-day news.
Reversed
A period of illness. Depending on other cards, seeking solace away from day-to-day events.

Ten of Swords
Depending where it falls, this card can be interpreted as you getting a kick in the teeth. Not literally, of course. Put simply, someone will be saying something nasty to you.
REVERSED
Sudden and unexpected changes that bring chaos.

Nine of Swords
This card means depression, again it depends where it falls in the spread as to who will be suffering the depression.
Reversed
Life gradually begins to improve.

Eights of Swords
Busy times brought about by unexpected news.
Reversed
Feeling as if you are being used.

Seven of Swords
Busy times.
Reversed
Certain circumstances will prevent you achieving your

aims.

Six of Swords
Making a longer journey than usual.
Reversed
Changes in travel plans.

Five of Swords
Worry.
Reversed
Uncertainty, lack of confidence.

Four of Swords
Illness.
Reversed
A curb on all activities.

Three of Swords
An upset.
Reversed
Deceit, treachery, discord.

Two of Swords
Relieved; something that has been worrying you reaches a conclusion.
Reversed
Acting on bad advice.

THE SUIT OF WANDS

The suit of wands represents work.

The Ace of Wands

The start of a new hobby or work project.

Reversed

False starts to do with work.

King of Wands

A man who is always motivated by work.

Reversed

An idle and lazy man.

Queen of Wands

This woman prefers to work rather than be at home.

Reversed

A woman who lacks motivation.

Knight of Wands

A message to do with work.

Reversed

Appointments to do with work being cancelled.

Page of Wands

Discussing a new hobby with a youngster.

Reversed

A superficial, arrogant person.

Ten of Wands

Tired and worn out due to overwork.
Reversed
Being too controlling and overbearing.

Nine of Wands
Feeling better, usually to do with work.
Reversed
Finding work stressful.

Eight of Wands
Confusion around a working condition.
This suit refers to the emotional side of our lives and deals with many aspects of it.

Seven of Wands
Opposition to plans.
Reversed
Things slowly turning your way.

Six of Wands
Successful end to a project.
Reversed
A delay in a working condition.

Five of Wands
Worry surrounds you.
Reversed
After a period of depression, life begins to improve.

Four of Wands
A win or a success.
Reversed
A work matter takes longer to resolve than you thought it would.

Three of Wands
Work offers.
Reversed
The failure of a work project.

Two of Wands
Completion of a work scheme with the help of someone else.
Reversed
A failure of a work idea due to lack of cooperation.

THE SUIT OF CUPS
Represents everything to do with the family.

Ace of Cups
Happiness around the home.
Reversed
Sadness brought about by emotional problems.

King of Cups
A kind generous man who loves his home.
Reversed

A man who lacks emotional stability.

Queen of Cups

This woman is a real home-maker and always puts her family first.

Reversed

A woman who dislikes domesticity.

Knight of Cups

Hearing news to do with family or friends.

Reversed

Receiving sad news to do with a relationship.

Page of Cups

Hearing news of a younger family member or friend.

Reversed

Unexpected changes taking place.

Ten of Cups

A happy family time.

Reversed

Disruption of plans.

Nine of Cups

Hearing news that pleases you.

Reversed

Taking professional advice to do with family issues.

Eight of Cups

In a situation where you change your mind.
Reversed
Plans fall through due to lack of interest.

Seven of Cups

Making important decisions surrounding your life.
Reversed
Fear of the unknown leads to arrangements being broken.

Six of Cups

The card of reminiscing. Whether they are happy memories depends on the surrounding cards.
Reversed
Indecision leads to confusion.

Five of Cups

Worry and strife.
Reversed
Trouble around the home.

Four of Cups

A time of boredom, unable to make decisions.
Reversed
Over-indulgence and false pride.

Three of Cups

Hearing of a happy event.
Reversed
Hearing of trouble to do with a birth.

Two of Cups

Meeting someone new. This does not necessarily mean the start of a new relationship; as with all cards, it depends on what cards surround it.

Reversed

A breakdown in a relationship.

THE SUIT OF PENTACLES

This card represents money and every financial aspect of your life.

Ace of Pentacles

Money you have not worked for coming your way, the amount you will receive depends on the surrounding cards.

Reversed

Self-indulgence, vanity, greed.

The King of Pentacles

A man who has a great love of money and financial matters.

Reversed

A greedy man who can only think of money.

The Queen of Pentacles

A woman who has a great knowledge of money matters.

Reversed

A woman who has allowed money to become her god.

Knight of Pentacles

Hearing unexpected news regarding money.
Reversed
Bad news regarding money.

Page of Pentacles
Discussing money with a younger person.
Reversed
Trouble around money to do with younger people.

Ten of Pentacles
Finances improving.
Reversed
A lack of money leads to depression.

Nine of Pentacles
Receiving a gift.
Reversed
Stolen goods.

Eight of Pentacles
The card of work.
Reversed
Loss of work due to inertia.

Seven of Pentacles
A failure of a working condition.
Reversed
Financial troubles.

Six of Pentacles
Giving out a gift; it could be a gift of money.
Reversed
Losing money unexpectedly.

Five of Pentacles
A loss of work.
Reversed
Job loss, not necessarily permanent; it could be due to illness or weather conditions.

Four of Pentacles
Pleased with the outcome of a project.
Reversed
Abandoning a project.

Three of Pentacles
Business offers.
Reversed
Failure of offers.

Two of Pentacles
Spending money. Depending on surrounding cards, a need to watch your spending habits.
Reversed
Reckless spending.

DOING A TAROT SPREAD
You will over the course of the coming months work

your own spreads out. I will briefly describe one of the readings I use.

THREE-MONTH READING

First shuffle and cut the cards, then deal seven cards and place them right to left on the work surface. Deal seven more cards and place them beneath the top row. Proceed in this manner until you have seven rows of seven cards.

Once this is completed, you are ready to begin your first reading.

It is important that you always read from right to left.

The top line of cards is always the past.

The following rows are not in any time line; whatever you see can happen immediately or at the end of the three months. This is good, in my opinion, as if you saw something bad coming up and knew when it was going to happen, you wouldn't bother getting up that day. It's important to point out that the majority of what you read in the cards will happen in a different way to how you think it will. Again, this is good as you should never let the cards rule your life. If a client says that you haven't given them the answer to their problem, point out that the answer probably is in the reading you have just given them, but the cards have decided to give them the answer in a different way. There again, there is the possibility that the time is not right for them to know the solution to their problem.

To read the six rows, start on row two and study the cards intently; a picture of what is going to happen will gradually emerge; follow the cards through by studying every single row. Be patient, take your time and let the whole spread speak to you. Each card within the three-month spread is linked to the other cards and has a story to tell you.

Should a client ask you when one of their relatives is going to die and are going to inherit their money (and at some point, someone will), inform them politely that this is something you never see. That isn't what tarot card readings are about.

Never tell a client that a relative is going to die, that is one of the worst things a reader can ever tell a customer. I remember a lady came to visit me one day when I did readings for the general public. She was distraught after being told her husband was going to die in a road accident. Her husband drove for a living, and she said every day when he left for work, she died a thousand deaths thinking she would never see him again. How you deal with a client who has been told something like this is extremely difficult. I read the cards for her and didn't see anything untoward happening to her or her family. I did my best to reassure her, but I knew the other reader's words were imprinted in her mind. I gave her the telephone number of a counsellor and also told her that it would take her a long time to leave that reading behind, but that she would eventually come to terms with it and move on.

Always tell your clients that you can only tell them what they put into the cards. Never hazard a guess because you could be wrong, and you will have lost a client. By telling the truth, you will gain their respect, and they will return repeatedly for readings and tell their friends that they trust you. This is how you build your reputation.

TELEVISION SHOWS

Over recent years, there has been an influx of psychic programmes on our televisions. These have proved to be extremely popular. One show in particular seems to have attracted an enormous audience. This is the show *'Most Haunted'*.

For some reason or other, it has really grabbed the nation's attention and it has spread round this country and others like a virus.

Now I'm all for entertainment, and this is how I've always viewed *'Most Haunted'*; as a good laugh, nothing else. I have never for one moment believed anything in it was true. I mean, to my mind, no self-respecting ghost is going to appear just because a television crew and a group of people turn up to film them. The trouble is thousands of people believe it is true and hang on to every word that is spoken.

This programme hasn't helped the serious ghost investigators in any way whatsoever. In fact, when I have spoken to some investigators, they say it has damaged their credibility, a great pity to say the least.

'Most Haunted' is listed as an entertainment show so how can it be taken seriously? It has raised the profile of psychic phenomena, but not in a favourable light, in my opinion.

Other programmes are aired along similar lines, but

without a live audience. *'Ghost Hunters'* is one such show, but like *'Most Haunted'* and other shows of the same ilk, it has a format, and the outcome is usually the same. In fact, I begin to know what the people are going to say before they say it.

Some of the television investigators try to have conversations with the ghost. Do they seriously believe that a ghost is going to reply to them? How remarkable that would be, but I don't think it will ever happen. If they did receive a ghostly reply, would I believe them?

TIME TRAVEL

Can people travel back in time, or even into the future?

I and many other people have experienced time slips. There are numerous books, films, and television programmes devoted to this fascinating subject, but so far, scientists have no conclusive proof showing that anyone has actually experienced it.

This, of course, doesn't mean no one has ever experienced a time slip.

I have a friend who has experienced a number of time slips and other strange happenings. One time slip occurred when he was out walking one evening and he actually found himself walking through the village where he lived in a different time. He was able to explain everything he saw in graphic detail. What an incredible experience! It led him to writing a story about it.

My mother-in-law also experienced the following

intriguing time slip.

ROSE COTTAGE, BROMSGROVE, WORCS
Time Slip

When my mother-in-law lived at a cottage in Catshill, Bromsgrove, Worcs. in the mid-1940s, she had this strange experience.

One afternoon she was putting Joy, my late sister-in-law, in her cot for her afternoon sleep. Suddenly, Mom knew she had done it in an earlier lifetime; she saw herself dressed in a long dress covered by a large white apron. Joy was dressed in long petticoats. Mom said she tried hard to hold on to this time slip, but couldn't. It lasted about two minutes. Rose Cottage was very old.

LYN'S THOUGHTS ON TIME TRAVEL

I go off onto my own planet many a time in my thoughts and imagination. It's as though I've time travelled, but of course, at times like that we still have the awareness that we are grounded on this planet. So that's just imagination taking us to another level.

I read the Philadelphia experiment when the USA was testing time travel. Apparently, quite a few sailors half disappeared. Their molecules travelled and other parts of them remained here. All of that was hushed up and I believe the experiments were abandoned.

Now, time slips, or windows, as I refer to them, I believe exist. I believe that there are other dimensions and that by chance a window can be stepped through, but when a person becomes frightened or confused by the surroundings, they slip back through the window. I believe that if we could raise our level of consciousness high enough, then we could utilise these windows at will. But humanity is very materialistic in general and fears the unknown simply because it is not viewed as a natural part of our existence.

MY TIME TRAVEL EXPERIENCE

This happened in the 1990s. It had been quite an ordinary evening in the summer. I had been chatting to an old friend about the supernatural.

John, my husband, was on nights and I went to bed at my normal time, read a romance novel, and settled down to sleep. As soon as my head touched the pillow, I felt myself being dragged down and down. The more I struggled against this unknown force, the more powerful it became. Suddenly I found myself on a street in London (don't ask me how I knew, I just did). There were two women walking in front of me in crinoline gowns and I knew it was my sister (she was still alive then) and me. They both looked behind, saw me, and screamed, as did I.

Immediately, the force grabbed me and dragged me ever upwards. My head was aching abominably by now and I felt so ill. This time, I was dragged upwards for a long period of time until I found myself in a beautiful garden. The grass was a vivid green and the flowers were wonderful. Then I saw John's grandfather, and some distance away was his grandmother. In that instance, I knew if they saw me, I would never return for they had both died a few years previously. All around me was an all-encompassing silence. Then I was dragged backwards again, spiralling down, and found myself back in bed, in shock with a powerful headache.

Strange? Yes, but it happened, and I wasn't asleep. The following morning, my friend popped in and as soon as he saw me, he asked what had happened. Well, it was to be expected really, with bags under my eyes and a haunted look. I mean, it was quite a scary experience.

I never forgot that strange happening and hoped it would never happen again. I like to be in control of situations and I had no control whatsoever when that happened. Try as I might, I couldn't escape from the all-powerful force that seemed to have taken over my body.

The cobblestone street in London was extremely wet and shiny and the dresses my sister and I were wearing were vivid in their colours. I felt the cold air around us and it was far from pleasant. I do remember that there was a lot of old straw lying around. In a way, I wished it had lasted longer so I had more to tell of the street scene.

I always wondered why John's grandparents appeared as sitting apart from each other. When I knew them, they were retired and spent every minute together and appeared to be very close indeed.

In later years, John's mom told me that in fact they had gone through a bad patch in their marriage and I wondered if this was what had led me to seeing them apart.

Jenny Cockell's book about her past life, which I

mentioned earlier, has always intrigued me and led me to believe that perhaps we do live other lifetimes. I know our genes are passed down through the generations, but I cannot say that we truly live again in this way. We ultimately become another person. In the lifetime I saw on the London Street, my sister and I were the same people. Apart from our clothing, we looked exactly as we did when we were younger in this lifetime.

LYN'S THOUGHTS ON MY TIME TRAVEL EXPERIENCE

That must have been a really strange and scary experience for you. It's hard for me to give an opinion because the experience was personal to you, and anyone who gives an opinion would be influenced by their own beliefs. However, I will do my best to be objective.

If you were a stranger, I would ask the following: Were you overtired, did you read a book before bedtime which may have influenced you; watched a film; had a very recent discussion about similar things to your experience? However, I know that at the time you were awake, and I would ask a stranger, could this have been a lucid dream. But, Carol, you *did* experience it, and as I've known you many years, I know that you know the difference between real events and ones that there is a reasoned answer to.

So what happened? You must have been Astral travelling? Or regressing?

It obviously gave you some distress, enough to recall it

clearly after all these years. It may have been one of those moments in time when the conditions were just right for you to slip back. You seemed to understand that you must not allow the grandparents to see you. Perhaps that was because you were given those moments as a gift to view the other side/other dimension/view through the window.

The following photographs are of a few of the haunted sites in Staffordshire, showing that numerous people see ghosts. This is further proof that ghosts exist.

Rugeley Town Centre – Many of the shops are haunted.

Rugeley Library, Staffordshire – The ghost of a lady dressed in a crinoline gown haunts the library.

The Vine Inn, Rugeley, Staffordshire – The above public house is haunted by the ghost of a coachman.

Hawkesyard Priory, Staffordshire – This ancient site is alleged to be haunted.

This beautiful old church is reputed to be haunted by a number of ghosts.

The ancient High House Stafford – A number of ghosts are said to haunt the High House.

Croxden Abbey, Staffordshire – Allegedly haunted by monks.

My dog – Boyden – He is extremely sensitive to psychic phenomena, as are many dogs.

Dominoes – These are sometimes used for prediction purposes as an aid to clairvoyance.

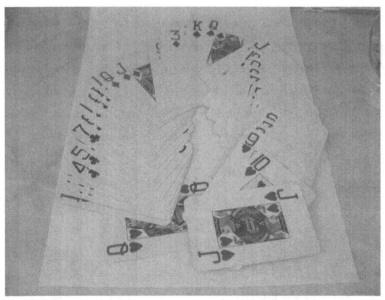

Playing Cards – Used to divine the future.

DREAMS

Experts tell us we all dream and that when we do, we are responding to our subconscious thoughts. Whatever has happened in our waking lives, we reinterpret it in our sleeping hours.

Much has been written over the years about dreaming, and many of the books describe the different stages of sleep.

For me, the most fascinating types of dreams are the ones that predict the future – or appear to. I've read many accounts of these. A lot of these dreams have foretold disasters that actually happened. I often wonder, what is the point of a dream that foretells a terrible air disaster or some awful tragedy, such as September 11th, when they cannot be prevented?

I've read that people who have had such dreams contact the authorities giving out warnings, only to be ignored, and then the disaster occurs. The poor recipient of the dream is then left wondering why they had the dream in the first place.

MY DREAM

One Sunday morning in the autumn of 1998, my husband and I were going to Lichfield to do some shopping. We decided to visit Fradley car boot sale first. As we were motoring along, I suddenly remembered a dream I had had the previous evening. Telling my husband about it, I said it had been about a man we had known for quite a while, but hadn't seen or even mentioned for about eight years. The dream was quite funny and strange in parts, as dreams often are, and we had quite a laugh about it. On reaching the boot sale, we were walking onto the site and who should we see but the person I had dreamt of. Although we were astonished, we had to laugh as we told him about the dream, and that we had just been talking about him. We often say how strange that was.

Yes, I believe that dreams can and do predict the future, but as with all things to do with the paranormal, we cannot alter what they tell us. What will be will be.

On the following pages are a few of my dream interpretations. I used the tarot cards and numerology to help me interpret the dream explanations. The ones listed are taken from a book of dreams that I wrote a few years ago.

It is best to use my dream interpretations as a starting point for your own explanation.

A

ACQUAINTANCES

Possible new meetings.

ACRIMONY

Bad feelings within the family. False friendships.

ACROBAT

Beware someone is using you.

Be careful of emotional blackmail.

ACTING

If you see yourself acting, this could well mean that you are deceiving yourself.

Stop trying to hide how you are feeling from the world.

ACUPUNCTURE

Beware of false friends.

ADDER

A woman will cause you trouble soon.

ADDICTED

You will be giving something up.

ADDING UP

Making decisions to alter your lifestyle.

ADDRESS

Possible move or holiday soon.

ADHERE

This dream is telling you to be more confident in your approach to life.

ADJUDICATING

Make sure someone isn't trying to boss you about.

ADJUSTING

Trouble around relationships.

ADMINISTRATING

Promotion on the horizon.

ADOPTING

A friend offers to help you.

ANGEL

Good dream - loyal and helpful friendships.

You have a guardian angel.

ANNOUNCING

Good news on the way.

ANORAK

A new hobby of the traditional kind.

ANOREXIA

A possible warning to check your diet.

ANTHEM

A need for orderliness.

ANTIBIOTIC

Confiding in a friend.

ANTIQUE

Reminiscing about the past.

ANTISEPTIC

This is the right time to heal a relationship.

APPETITE

Meeting life head-on.

APPOINTMENT

Check all diary dates to ascertain they are correct.

ARCHES

Stop being indecisive.

ARMCHAIR

Take a short break.

ARTIST

Become more outgoing, but also a warning to be careful.

ASS

Avoid embarrassing situations.

ATLAS

Looking up old friends.

ATTENDANT

Concentrate on one thing at a time.

AUCTIONEER

An indication not to take any chances where money is concerned.

AUDIENCE

Perhaps finding yourself in the spotlight.

More often than not, this dream indicates an improvement in your circumstances.

AUNT

Dreaming of a family member means that someone in your family will be taking professional advice.

AUTHOR

Finances will begin to improve over the coming months.

B

BABBLE

Quarrels within the family.

BABIES

Your dream is reflecting an inner desire to get out and about.

BABOON

Someone will be out to cause you mischief.

BACHELOR

New meetings.

BACKACHE

It could well be predicting an illness.

BACKFIRE

Plans go awry.

BACKSEAT

You need to be more outgoing, i.e. stop hiding from life.

BADGER

Hiding from problems.

BADMINGTON

A new hobby.

BAG

Look after your possessions.

BAGPIPES

Finding yourself in a noisy situation.

BAIT

Someone looking for you.

BAKER

A need for home comforts.

Feeling insecure in a relationship.

BALCONY

Perhaps over-reaching yourself.

BALD

If you saw yourself as being bald this means a lack of self-respect.

If it was someone else, then this person will be

approaching you for advice.

BALE

Wrapping your troubles away? Stop hiding from the truth.

BAND

You will hear of a celebration.

BANQUET

A celebration.

BAPTISM

Finding yourself in a new situation.

BARN

Rebuilding your life.

BARRICADE

A need for you to take professional advice to help sort out your emotional life.

BAT

Take care with a relationship.

BATTLE

A family argument.

BEAD

Try to slow down.

BEAK

Someone will be nasty to you.

BEANS

A good energetic time ahead.

BEAR

Perhaps you have been feeling lonely of late and the bear is symbolic of hugs and cuddles.

BEAUTY

Poor self-image.

BEAVER

A lot of hard work ahead.

BED

Watch your health.

BEDBUGS

Outsiders will try to cause trouble.

BED LINEN

Unexpected changes in your home life will soon take place.

BEDROOM

Feeling insecure.

BEES

A busy time ahead.

BEER

A celebration.

BEETROOT

Signs of suppressed anger.

BEGGAR

Look after finances.

BELT

If tight, relax more.

BENCH

Empty? Try to mix more.

BILLS

An easing of money circumstances.

BILLIARDS

Taking up some kind of recreation.

BINGO

Some kind of success with finances.

BIRO

If you were using the biro, it's a sign that you need to catch up on a work issue.

BIRTHMARK

Emotional turmoil surrounds you.

BLUEBELL

Summer will be a promising time for you.

BLUSHING

Finding yourself in a difficult situation.

BOARDING HOUSE

Difficult time financially.

BOARDING SCHOOL

Feeling emotionally separated from friends and family.

BOIL

Anger will surround you.

BOLTS

A fear of being locked up.

BOMB

Anger surrounds you.

BONE

Taken literally, someone will have a bone to pick with you.

BOOKS

New learning.

BRIDE

Shortly hear of a wedding.

BRIDEGROOM

New relationship.

BRIDESMAID

Changes in a relationship.

BRIDLE

A case of you can lead a horse to water, but you can't make him drink.

BRISTLE

Anger will surround you.

BROADCASTING

Finding yourself in an unexpected situation.

BUBBLES

A surprise - perhaps a short break.

BUCKET

Someone will be getting upset with you.

BUILDINGS

A muddled dream; a fear of finding yourself trapped, i.e. claustrophobia.

BULL

Someone you know will cause trouble in a personal matter.

BUSH

Hiding from the world.

BUS STOP

Show caution in relationships.

BUTCHER

Trouble around a working condition.

BUTTER

False friends.

BUTTON

Reconsolidations.

C

CABIN

Making important decisions about your life.

CABLE

Reminiscing about living in the past.

The dream is telling you that now is the time to move on.

CAFE

New meetings.

Possibility of someone important entering your life.

CAGE

Opposition to plans.

CAKE

Good news.

CALENDAR

A sign to look after your health.

CALF

The start of a new hobby.

CALL

Visiting clubs.

CAMEL

Disappointing news regarding a project.

CAMELLIA

An excellent dream. There is a lot of excitement ahead for you.

CAMEO

Good news to do with finances.

CAMERA
Good ideas creatively; an inspirational dream indicating that all your plans will knit together.

CAMPING
Receiving a surprise.

CANCEL
Disappointing news.

CANE
Insight into a dilemma that has been worrying you.

CANNON
Unexpected news that could be life changing.

CANOPY
A lot of news will be heading your way.

CANTEEN
Arguments.

CAP
Finances improving.

CAPE
Try to avoid disappointments.

CAPTAIN
Confusion surrounds you.

Indication to take professional advice.

CAPTIVE
Success is imminent.

CAPTURE
Fear of the unknown.

CARAVAN
Hangers-on.

Best to clear away any emotional debris you may have.

CARD

Making plans for your future, i.e. work-wise.

CARDBOARD

Making firm decisions about your life.

CARDIGAN

A need for re-assurance within a relationship.

CARETAKER

Looking for a family figure to help you along the way.

CARGO

Re-organization.

CARNATION

Sad times ahead.

A refusal from someone near to you.

CARP

Good times ahead.

CARPENTER

A need to re-structure your life and be more positive.

CARPET

Overdoing things.

CARRIER BAG

Other people's worries will weigh you down.

CARROT

Success with the help of someone else.

CARRY COT

Predicting the future or being in need of help yourself.

CARTOON

Successes and gains.

CARTWHEEL

Finding yourself in a confusing situation.

CARVE

Determined to make a success of life.

CASE

Travelling.

CASH

Money coming your way.

CASSEROLE

A relationship matter will be resolved satisfactorily.

CASSETTE

Good news.

CATALOGUE

Seeking new horizons.

CATHERINE WHEEL

Spinning confusion surrounds you.

CATWALK

Hiding from life, i.e. a sign to get out and about.

CAVE

Feelings of restrictions within the family.

CEMENT

An awkward situation will arise.

Take extra care with plans.

CEMETERY

Not what it seems. New beginnings for you.

CERTIFICATE

Something you've been aiming for will be successful.

CHAIR

A need for comfort.

CHALET

A need for comfort.

CHALK

Meeting someone new.

CHEMIST

Professional advice.

CHEQUE-CARD

A warning to take extra care of your valuables.

CHERRY

A good dream as it heralds new learning.

CHEESE

Careful planning will bring good results.

CHEW

Spreading good news.

CHILD

Family news.

CHIME

Hearing of a family wedding.

CHIMNEYS

A need to keep your feet on the ground.

CHIMPANZEE

True love.

CHINA

If broken, a break up; if whole, a coming together.

CHIP

Broken friendships.

CLAIRVOYANT

Taking professional advice regarding your lifestyle.

CLAPPING

Seeing a show or achieving something you've set your sights on.

CLAW

Trouble ahead.

CLIFF

Take time out to research something you aim to take up.

CLINIC

Offers coming your way.

CLOAK

Try to stop hiding from life.

CLOCK

Feeling as if life's passing you by.

Overdoing it. Under stress - a warning to slow down.

CLOTHES

A change of clothing to a new outfit represents a need you have to restructure your lifestyle.

COINS

Counting the cost, not necessarily financially.

COLD

Illness.

COMB

If using, trying to straighten out a romance.

COMMITTEE

Taking advice.

COMPLIMENT

Praise from an unexpected source.

COMPUTER

New - learning or a new job.

CONCERN

Troubled times.

CONCERT

Outings.

CONCRETE

Solid friendships.

CONKER

Try not to be overlooked.

CONSERVATORY

Perhaps having one, or new plans for the garden.

CONVICT

Someone from the past will be in touch.

COOKING

Someone will be making plans on your behalf.

COPPER

Trouble around money matters.

COPYING

A need to assert yourself.

COOKIES

A friend will be asking advice.

CORAL

A need to protect yourself against unfortunate happenings.

CORK

A celebration to come.

CORN

Happiness in the autumn.

CORRESPONDENCE

It means exactly what you dreamt - a lot of communications around you.

CORRIDOR

If you were running along the corridors then this

represents your waking life.

It's as if you are totally lost in troubles of your own making.

CORSET

Easing of a situation that has concerned you.

COSTUMES

A façade, i.e. be your real self.

COSTUME JEWELLERY

This could be telling you that some of your friends are fake.

COT

A need for emotional security.

COTTAGES

Seeking comfort.

COUCH

Perhaps you should ease up.

COUGHING

It could be a sign of illness, a warning to take care.

COUNTING

Missing an appointment, i.e. slow down.

COUSIN

Discussions around family matters.

CRAB

Beware of false friendships.

CRADLE

News of a happy event.

CRANE

Aiming too high.

CRASH

Plans moving forward.

CRATE

Upsets within the family.

CREAM

Doing well, succeeding.

CROCHET

Mind someone doesn't stitch you up.

CROCKS

If broken, trouble around a relationship.

If whole, cementing a broken relationship.

CROCUS

Laughter.

CROW

Unpleasant news.

CROWN

Achieving your aims.

CRYING

Sadness surrounds you or a family member.

CRYSTAL

Healing.

CUCKOO

Jealousy

CUCKOO CLOCK

Jealousy.

CUP

If the cup is full, you will be achieving your ambition.

If it is empty, it will take longer than you thought to achieve your ambition.

CUPID

A new relationship.

CURRY

Hearing some gossip.

CURTAIN

If closed, the dream means the ending of a relationship.

If open, a new relationship will start.

CUTLERY

Trouble with relationships.

CYCLING

If you are travelling uphill, there's a struggle ahead for you.

Going downhill means matters that have worried you will be resolved.

D

DOCUMENTS

Perhaps a legal matter will be needing your attention soon.

DUST

A need to get rid of the negativity that surrounds you.

E

EAR

Someone is jealous of you.

EARTH

Unsettled times.

EATING

A sign you long for a close companion.

EDGE
Things will be looking up for you soon.
EDITING
A need to get your life in order.
EELS
Plans for travel will be made.
EFFIGY
Being creative but not in a positive way.
EGGS
A woman will interfere with your plans.
EGGSHELL
Trouble around plans.
EIGHT
A positive number to dream about.
EIGHTEEN
A propitious number; this is telling you something good will happen soon.
EIGHTY
A propitious number; this is telling you something good will happen soon.
ELASTIC
A fortunate dream. You seem to be reeling in good luck.
ELECTING
Seeking professional help.
ELECTRIC
Ascertain that your house is in order.
ELECTRONIC
A male member of the family will be starting a new career.

ELDER

Opposite meaning - trouble with the young.

ELEVEN

Good fortune.

ELF

All things mystical.

Researching the paranormal.

ELOPING

A sign you should face up to problems.

EMBARRASSED

Try to be more outgoing.

EMBASSY

A need to be more diplomatic.

EMBRACE

Lacking in affection.

EMBROIDERY

Taking control of your life.

EMBRYO

Too much looking back - be positive - look ahead.

EMERALDS

Jealousy surrounding you.

EMERGENCY

Opposite - a period of calm for you.

EMIGRANT

Looking ahead.

EMPRESS

News of a birth.

ENAMEL

A hard time ahead.

ENCORE

Something that happened in the past will recur.

END

A new beginning.

ENEMY

New friendship.

ENGAGE

News of friends getting married shortly.

ENGLISH

A lot of correspondence for a long time to come.

ENGRAVE

Taking up opportunities.

ENTERTAINING

A sign you should mix more often.

EXERCISE

Taking up a new hobby or the need to take advice.

EXHIBITION

New beginnings, new happenings, exciting times to come.

EXPLORE

The dream is advising you to get out and about more.

EYELASHES

Choose your friends carefully.

F

FABRIC

New starts, new beginnings.

FACECLOTH

Trying to sort your troubles out.

FACTORY

A need for tranquillity.

FAIL

Stop worrying - you will succeed.

FAINT

Feeling out of control of your life.

If you are feeling out of sorts, obviously it makes sense to see your doctor.

FAIRGROUND

Outings of a pleasurable kind.

FAIRIES

All things mystical.

FAIRY LIGHTS

Lighten up and realize that despite the down times the ups do happen more often.

FAKE

Do not be so trusting of everyone.

FALCON

Shows you are a responsible person.

FALLING

Feeling your life is running out of control; a warning to step back, slow down, or trouble will occur.

FALLING OUT

Opposite meaning to what it says. This dream means a coming together.

FAMILY

A good dream when you see yourself surrounded by family.

FARM

Meeting new people.

FASHION

Dreaming of fashion shows you have a lot of self-confidence.

FATE

You cannot alter what lies ahead.

FAT

Did you see yourself as fat? If so, and you're not overweight, then stop worrying about your diet!

FATIGUED

A warning to slow down.

FEAR

Worrying.

FEAST

Watch your diet.

FENCES

Relatives or acquaintances will be in touch.

FERRET

Troubled times ahead.

FEVER

Feeling low in health and spirit.

FIREGUARD

Feeling low in health and spirit.

FIREMAN

Taking professional advice.

FIREWORKS

News of squabbles.

FISH

Unexpected good luck.

FLAG

It could be an indication of a celebration coming up shortly.

FLAME

Someone you admired in the past will be in touch.

FLAMINGO

Good luck.

FLARE

Trouble around a journey.

FLOATING

Feeling your life is running out of control; a warning to step back, slow down, or trouble will occur.

FLOOR

Loyal friends.

FLYING

Feeling your life is running out of control; a warning to step back, slow down, or trouble will occur.

FLYING SAUCER

Discussions about UFOs.

G

GABLE

An upturn in your fortunes.

GADGET

New beginnings - hobbies - crafts.

GAFF

Reconciliation.

GAIN

Finances improving.

GALA

An extrovert entering your life.

GALAXY

New interests of a spiritual nature.

GALE

Hearing some bad news.

GALLEON

A warning to you to watch your finances.

GALLERY

You will be receiving some extra attention.

GAMBLE

A warning not to make changes.

GAMBOL

Becoming involved with children.

GAME

An enjoyable time ahead.

GAMMON

Talking good sense.

GANG

Meetings with groups of people.

GANG PLANK

Stop sailing so close to the wind, probably in business affairs.

GANGWAY

A long-standing problem will be resolved.

GANNET

Keep a tight rein on your purse strings, i.e. do not lend or give any money to anyone soon.

GAOL

Suffering from stress.

GARAGE

A lot of hard work ahead.

Moving home is a possibility.

GARBAGE

A sign you need to make changes to your lifestyle.

GARDENER

Jack-of-all-trades, master of none.

GARLAND

Many short trips.

GARMENT

Disguising the truth.

Stop hiding from yourself.

GARRISON

Someone taking your side in a disagreement.

GARROTTE

Sudden end to a friendship.

GAS

Hearing untruths.

GATEAU

Try to be more positive.

GATECRASHER

Beware of false friendships.

GATE KEEPER

New relationship.

GATE POST

New home.

GAUNTLET

Giving up.

Be more positive.

GAUGE

Repairing a friendship.

GAWP

Finding yourself in a ridiculous situation.

GIN

Taking time out.

GINGER

Someone losing their temper.

GIPSY

A longing to escape and be more carefree.

GIRAFFE

Someone watching out for you.

GIRDLE

Collecting money that is owed to you.

GIRL

A new member coming into the family.

GIRO

To dream about money is fortuitous.

GIVING

Reminder to check your birthday book.

GIVING UP

Giving up.

Be more positive.

GLACIAL

Tricky situations arising.

GLADIATOR
Fighting someone else's battles for them.

GLAMOROUS
Worrying about your appearance.

GLARE
Finding yourself in a ridiculous situation.

GLASS
Shy, always keeping a low profile.

GLAZIER
A smooth -talking individual entering your life.

GLEAM
Fresh hopes.

GLITTERING
Remember all that glitters is not gold.

H

HACKING
Putting someone in their place.

HACKSAW
All will not be as it seems.

HADDOCK
Unexpected good luck.

HAGGARD
A warning to slow down.

HAGGLING
It means what it says: trying hard to get a bargain.

HAIL
To dream you are caught in a hailstorm shows you feel you lack affection in a relationship.

HAIR

Feeling as if you have lost your self-respect.

HAIRBRUSH

Sorting out your emotional life.

HAIRCUT

Feeling as if you have lost your self-respect.

HAIRPIECE

Trying to regain confidence.

HALL

Losing direction.

HALLOWEEN

Dealing with all matters spiritual.

HAMMER

Unexpected visitors arrive.

HAMMOCK

Dreaming of past times.

HAMPER

Invitations arriving soon.

HEADBAND

Tight corners.

HEADDRESS

Predicting a wedding.

HEADMASTER

Taking some form of professional advice.

HEADQUARTERS

Longing for homely surroundings.

HEADSET

A need for security.

HEART

Doing charity work.

HEATHER

Good luck dream.

HEAT WAVE

Finding yourself in trouble.

HEAVEN

Peace will follow conflict.

HEAVY

Life getting you down for a while.

HEDGE

A need for security.

HEDGEHOG

Finding yourself in an uncomfortable situation.

HILL

Difficult times ahead.

HONEY

A gathering of friends.

HONEYMOON

Predicting holidays.

HOOD

Are you hiding from the truth in a situation?

HOOK

Romantic entanglements.

HOOPLA

In a winning situation.

HOP

Indecisive.

HORSE
Always a good dream; it shows you have good friends.

HOUSES
There could be a house move on the cards.

HUGGING
A new romance for the unattached.

HUNTING
Worry surrounds you.

HUT
Insecurities surround you.

HYACINTH
New beginnings in the spring.

HYENA
Decisions to be made about money matters.

HYMN
Pleasant news.

HYPNOTIST
Taking some kind of advice.

HYPODERMIC NEEDLES
Take care who you socialise with, or you could land in trouble.

I

ICE
Something you have been longing to happen will come about shortly.

ICING
Good news.

ICON

People respect you.

ID CARD

New people entering your life.

IDIOT

New courses taken up.

IGLOO

Need for constant reassurance.

IGNITION

Finding yourself more in control, i.e. more confident.

ILL

Improving circumstances.

ILLUMINATIONS

Holidays on the horizon.

ILLUSIONS

Life will be difficult for a short while.

IMITATING

Compliments.

IMPORT

Losing something.

IMPOVERISHED

Some successes and gains.

IMPULSIVE

Warning to slow down.

Watch your finances.

INCENSE

Matters relating to religion will be discussed.

INCOMPLETE

Be more positive.

Finish one project before starting another.

INCUBATOR

Foretelling a happy event.

Becoming more positive.

INDIGESTION

Upsets in your emotional life.

INDIGO

Depression surrounds you.

INDISCREET

Be careful who you put your trust in.

INDISTINCT

Puzzling matters will eventually be sorted out.

INDUSTRIOUS

A warning to slow down.

INFANT

Talks concerning children and family matters.

INJECTION

Fear of the unknown.

INJURY

It could be a warning to take extra care.

INSOMNIA

Athletics.

INSULT

There will be some disturbances in your life soon.

INSURANCE

Check everything is up to date concerning your insurance.

INTERVIEWING

New job or home.

INVADED
Unexpected happenings.
INVITATION
Receiving unexpected invitations.
INVOICE
A long-standing money matter will be resolved.
IOU
Money matters easing.
IRIS
Good news around summertime.
ISLAND
Withdrawal.
IVORY
A friend is not being totally truthful with you.
IVY
Someone is too dependent on you emotionally, i.e. try to stand back a little and let them take responsibility for their own lives.

J

JABBING
Worry needlessly.
JACKDAW
Take care of personal possessions.
JACKET
Wrapping up a business deal.
JACK IN THE BOX
A surprise in store.

JACKPOT

You could be receiving a windfall.

JADE

A friend will be envious of your good luck.

JAIL

Inner struggles.

JAM

Finding yourself in an uncomfortable situation.

JANITOR

Someone confiding a secret in you.

JASMINE

A new relationship is about to happen for you.

JAVELIN

Be aware that someone will be causing you trouble.

JAYWALKING

A warning to stop daydreaming and open your eyes to reality.

JAZZ

Feeling happy.

JEALOUSY

It could be someone is jealous of you.

JEERING

The opposite to this is true. People value your opinions.

JERSEY

Seeking security.

JEWELS

Receiving a gift.

JIGSAW

You will literally be fitting the pieces of your life back together.

JILTED

A warning of a split in a relationship.

JOCKEY

Someone trying to push you out of the way.

JOURNAL

Telling you to make notes of all you do. This is an important dream.

JOURNEY

This dream could be predicting the future, a warning perhaps to ensure all is in order before you start out. Alternatively, starting a new way of life.

JUDGE

Criticism will be directed at you, by someone you know.

JUDO

Good news.

JUGGLE

Finally achieving your dream after a struggle.

JUMBLE

An indication something in your life needs attention.

JUNCTION

At a crossroads in your life.

JUNE

Dreaming of a particular month of the year indicates probable changes in your circumstances.

JUNGLE

A need to resolve your problems.

JURY

Criticism will be levelled at you.

L

LABEL

Determination.

LABORATORY

Investigating a problem.

LABOUR

Work offers.

LABRADOR

Patience and calm needed.

LABYRINTH

Confusion will surround you in the near future.

LACE

A bit like a spider's web - finding yourself in a tangle.

LACQUER

A tricky situation will arise.

LADYBIRD

Hearing of changes.

LAME

Overcoming problems.

LAMP

Someone will be helping you see a way out of your difficulties.

LAMPPOST

Success and gains coming your way.

LAMPSHADE

Hearing some gossip.

LANDLADY

Help given by a stranger.

LARVA

A few family squabbles ahead.

LASER

Happier times coming your way.

LATE

This could be a warning dream. Take care in whatever you do soon.

LAUGHING

Happiness.

LAUNDRETTE

Getting rid of problems.

LAW

Be careful who you trust.

LAWN

Family outings.

LAWYER

A sign you should put your affairs in order.

LEADER

A dream that shows you are a confident person.

LEAVING

It signals the end of a relationship.

LEDGERS

Sorting out every aspect of your life.

LEGACY

Not necessarily money coming to you; more than likely a warning to be careful when dealing with financial matters.

LEGAL

Problems will be resolved after a lot of wrangling.

LEGGINGS

Feeling a need for security.

LEMON

Offers not quite to your liking coming your way.

LEOPARD

Be wary of strangers.

LEOTARD

New meetings to do with a working condition.

LETTERS

Hearing important news.

LEVEL CROSSING

Take care, you are at an important point in your life. Be careful when making decisions.

LIAR

Finding someone out in deceit.

LIBRARY

A new learning or doing research.

LIFEBELT

Help from an unexpected quarter.

LIGHT

Feeling the need to escape your personal problems.

LIGHT BULB

Full of good ideas.

LIGHTHOUSE

Extending a welcome.

LILAC

A relaxing time ahead.

LIMOUSINE

Taking a step up the ladder, i.e. promotion.

LINE DANCING

Order and regularity.

LINER

Talks around holiday plans.

LINESMAN

Someone trying to take charge of you.

LION

Professional help will be sought.

LISPING

Indecision surrounds you.

LISTS

Order and regularity will rule the day.

LITTER

Confusion will surround you.

A hint to tidy up your emotional life.

LOFT

Problems resolved.

LOG

Good friendships.

LOOM

Acting out fantasies.

LOST

If you dreamt that you are lost, the dream is telling you to seek help with your emotional difficulties.

LOTTERY

It could be predicting a win.

LUNCH

Perhaps a warning that you need to take a break.

LUPIN

It indicates that you are a loyal person.

LUXURY

You will find the means to have that bit of extra luxury.

M

MACARONI

Receiving an unexpected gift.

MACHINERY

Ruffling a few feathers if you're not careful.

MAGAZINE

You will be doing research.

MAGGOTS

Beware who you trust.

MAGISTRATE

Taking charge of a difficult situation.

MAGNET

Attracting others to you.

MAGNIFYING GLASS

Taking a closer look at your life.

MAIL

Busy times ahead.

MAKE UP

Disguising not only your outward appearance, but also your innermost thoughts.

MALLET

Taking on too many responsibilities.

MAN

Perhaps a new friendship ahead.

MANDOLIN

Money coming your way.

MANNEQUIN

Travel involved with a happy event.

MANSION

Correspondence with authority.

MANUSCRIPT

It could be you have a hidden desire to write.

MARATHON

Stop trying to run away from your troubles.
Slow down.

MARCHING

A huge surprise in store for you.

MARKET

Visiting clubs, events, etc.

MASK

Stop hiding from yourself and problems will soon be resolved.

MAT

Symbolic - wiping away your troubles.

MATERIAL

Start of a new job, which will bring about financial gain.

MAUVE

All will not be as it appears.

MEDICINE

The start of something new.

MELON

Plans temporarily held up, but they will eventually be fulfilled.

MEMORIES

Longing for the past.

METEORITE

Hearing favourable news.

METERS

New meetings.

Alternatively, a lifting of depression.

MICROSCOPE

Disappointments to do with a working condition.

Arguments.

MILDEW

Old friends will be in touch.

MILK

The need for love and security in your life.

MILL

The wheel of fortune is turning in your favour.

MINIATURE

Take a look at your life. Does it need more putting into it?

MINISTER

You could soon be taking advice.

MIRACLE

Good luck ahead.

MIRACLE

Fantasy land.

MIRROR

Reflections of your innermost thoughts.

MISCHIEF

Trouble ahead, probably from youngsters.

MISS

Take advantage of offers.

MITTEN

Looking for comfort.

MOANING

Hearing good news.

MOB

Looking for new horizons.

MOCKING

Trouble from an acquaintance.

MONSOON

Storm clouds gathering, trouble within the family.

MOON

Getting involved with psychic phenomena.

MORNING

New beginnings.

MOSS

Someone clinging to you.

MOTH

Too many relationships.

A need to settle down.

MOTHER

Strong family ties.

MOUNTAIN

Life seems to be an uphill struggle.

MOURN

Need to get out and about.

MOUSE

Bad news.

MOVING

It depends; it could be troubles around a contract to do with a house move or work.

MUD

Don't get stuck in a rut.

MURDER

Be very careful who you trust.

MUSEUM

Research for a new project.

MUSHROOM

Things going well.

MUSIC

If loud, a need for you to quieten down and take things easy.I

If calm, a more settled time ahead.

MUSIC BOX

Nostalgia.

MUSTARD

Sharp words around you.

MUTTERINGS

Disturbances.

MUZZLE

Feeling too restricted emotionally.

MYSTIC

Interest in the supernatural.

N

NAGGING

Finding yourself in an unpleasant situation.

NAIL

Breaking free.

NAKED

Lack of self-respect.

NAP

A signal to slow down.

NAPKIN

Two meanings: hearing of a happy event or sending out invitations.

NATIVITY

It means what it says, i.e. you will shortly take part in some kind of religious festival.

NAVIGATING

Someone trying to take charge of your life.

You need more self-confidence.

NODDING

Finding a solution to your problems.

NOISE

A lot of correspondence will surround you.

NOOSE

A relationship becomes too cloying.

NOTE

Someone asking for your advice.

NOVEL

Someone new entering your life.

NURSE

Taking advice.

NURSERY SCHOOL

Interacting with children.

NUTS

Talks about buying and selling.

O

OAK

A good dream. You will be relieved that at long last things appear to be going your way.

OARS

Finding your way out of a difficult situation with a friend's help.

Alternatively, if it's just you who are using the oars, matters will take longer to resolve.

OFFICE

A desire for orderliness in your working life.

OFFICER

You need to take advice.

OIL

If the oil is swirling, troubled times ahead-

Rainbow effects - good news or sorting out an argument.

OIL PAINTING

A need for more creativity in your life.

OILSKIN

Talks about depression within the family.

OINTMENT

A time for healing.

ONE

A very powerful number. Things will certainly be changing for you in the very near future.

ONION

Mixed fortunes.

OPAL

Unlucky.

OPERA

A need for restraint with financial matters.

OPERATION

Concerns for a family member.

ORANGE

Surrounded by the warmth of loyal friends.

ORCHESTRA

A romantic dream.

ORDER

Success coming your way.

OUIJA BOARD

All things spiritual.

Alternatively a warning to leave well alone.

OUTFIT

Life is improving.

OVERALL

Covering up.

OVERBOARD

Taking too many chances.

OVERCOAT

Trying to hide from your troubles.

OVERTAKE

A warning that you need to slow down.

OVERTIME

Decisions around life.

OVERWEIGHT

Once you stop worrying about your self-image, you will be on the road to sorting the problem out.

OWL

A good dream. Things going better for you.

OYSTER

An unusual gift heading your way.

P

PACKING

Fresh starts, new beginnings.

Changes going on around you.

PADDLE

Worry surrounds you.

A time for reviewing your life.

PADLOCK

A release from emotional problems.

PAGES

Frightened that life is passing you by.

PAIN

Check your health.

PAINTING

It could be the start of a new business or hobby.

PALACE

Things improving in unexpected ways.

PALETTE

Some expensive times ahead.

PALMISTRY

All things mystical.

Alternatively, new meetings.

PANCAKE

Discussions around a personal matter.

PANDAS

Some unpleasant news.

PANEL

Good news.

PANIC

A warning to slow down.

PANSY

Someone from the past re-enters your life.

PANTHER

Adapting to changes; circumstances altering swiftly.

PANTOMIME

Perhaps you are always acting out a part instead of showing your true identity to the world.

PAPER

Good dream.

PARAPET

Worry.

PARK

Have you been feeling confined of late?

Dreaming of a park shows that your circumstances will improve shortly.

PARLIAMENT

A need for more order in your life.

PARROT

Gossip.

PARTING

As it says, a split in a close relationship.

PARTNER

Meeting someone new.

PEACOCK

Like Joseph's coat of many colours, don't be deceived by a flamboyant person in your life.

PEAT

Finding yourself in a claustrophobic situation.

PECK

Someone sharing a secret with you.

PEEL

Trouble.

PEN

Someone will be in touch by letter.

PENTHOUSE

Looking forward to succeeding.

PEOPLE

At times, you feel overwhelmed by people always laying their troubles at your door.

PERFUME

Success will soon be yours.

PERSPIRATION

Finding yourself in an uncomfortable situation.

PEST

Someone trying to annoy you. Keep your cool.

PETROL

Planning an excursion.

PHOTOCOPIER

Someone copying you.

PHYSIOTHERAPY

Taking advice.

PICKLE

Finding yourself in a muddle.

PILL

Feeling under the weather. This dream is advising you to seek help.

PILLAR-BOX

Communications.

PILLOW

Stop overdoing things.

PILOT

A need to get your life organised.

PIN

Uncertainty surrounds you. Try to settle down in your job and personal relationships.

PINEAPPLE

Take time out to indulge yourself in fanciful dreams and then go out and make them happen.

PINK

A need for affection in your life.

PIP

Someone making fun of you. The best thing to do is ignore them.

PIPE

You will be seeking comfort from someone in your close circle.

PIT

Feeling depressed.

PLANT

New life, new beginnings.

PLATFORM

Feeling as if no one listens to your problems.

PLAY

Good times ahead.

POISON

Someone close is deceiving you.

POSTMAN

A lot of news surrounds you.

POTATO

A stable relationship.

POTTER'S WHEEL

Good fortune.

PREGNANT

Looking forward to your future and making plans with a loved one.

PRESCRIPTION

A warning to check your health.

PRISON

A need to get out and about as your life has become stagnant.

PRIZE

Success.

PROBLEM

Helping a friend.

PRODUCER

You will be awarded a promotion and find yourself taking charge, and perhaps demonstrating how things are done.

PROFESSOR

Seeking advice from a higher authority.

PSYCHICS

Taking spiritual advice.

PSYCHIATRIST

Advice on an emotional matter.

PUDDLE

If murky, mixed emotions.I

If clear, a small worry will resolve itself.

PUNCTURE

Something taking longer than expected will eventually be completed.

PUPPET

Advising you to do your own thing.

PURSE

A warning to look after your finances.

PUZZLES

A lot of confusion around you.

PYJAMAS

Hearing of a change of address.

PYRAMID

A spiritual dream.

PYTHON

If it was coiled, be wary of strangers.

Q

QUAKER

A more settled time ahead.

QUARRY

A good dream, particularly if the quarry was full of stones.

QUEEN

Meeting somebody quite important who will be instrumental in bringing about changes in your life.

QUILT

A longing for security.

QUIZ

Are you the winner? If so, success lies ahead for you.

If losing, a sign that you need to be more positive.

R

RABBIT

In the company of a group of friends.

Alternatively, hearing some gossip.

RADIATOR

A need for a secure and loving relationship.

RADIO

Feeling left out.

RAFFLE

Taking too many chances. Slow down and enjoy your life.

RAFT

Not being responsible for your own life.

You feel as if life is passing you by.

RAGS

Is this an indication of how you see yourself? I.e. ill used.

RAILWAY

Predicting a holiday or a parting.

RAIN

A good dream.

RAINBOW

Sunshine after a bad time.

RAKE

Sorting out every aspect of your life.

RAMBLING

A suggestion to take time out away from home and work.

RAMP

Some difficulties to overcome.

RAPIDS

This dream is advising you not to let life get away from you.

RAT

Watch who you confide in.

RATTLE

Unexpected news.

READING

Possibly predicting a good result from an examination.

ROOM

If the room is empty, this represents how you feel about your life.

If the room is full of furniture, things will begin to go in your direction.

ROPE

A fortuitous dream; a dream of plenty.

ROULETTE

Signal not to take risks.

RUBBISH

Stand back and take stock of your emotional life.

RUBBLE

Stand back and take stock of your emotional life.

RUIN

Take advice before speculating, i.e. don't put all your eggs in one basket.

RULER

Making decisions to follow a new path through life.

RUNNING

Perhaps feeling as if your life is out of control.

S

SADDLE

Someone offering to help you with a work project.

SALAD

Mixed fortunes.

SALE

Expensive times ahead.

SALESMAN

Taking your pick from many admirers.

SALT

Good luck.

SAMPLER

Past times, i.e. nostalgia.

SANDCASTLE

Dreams and plans fulfilled.

SANDWICH

A hunger for more to happen in your life.

SATAN

Be careful who you trust.

SAUCER

If a teacup is resting on it, contentment.

If not, there is trouble ahead.

SAUNA

This dream is telling you that you need to unwind and relax.

SAW

Someone causing trouble for you.

SCALDED

Frictions within the family.

SCANNER

Worrying about exposure.

SCARECROW

Unexpected visitors arriving.

SCISSORS

A split in a relationship.

SCREAMING

Be careful who you trust.

SÉANCE

New interests in the paranormal.

SEASHELL

Good sign.

SEAT BELT

A warning to tighten up all round.

SECRET

Becoming more outgoing and confident.

SEER

Dealing with spiritual matters.

SEESAW

Emotional ups and downs.

SHARKS

A man will make accusations against you.

SHAVING

Important new beginnings.

SHEARS

A long dispute will be settled.

SHED

Changes in your lifestyle.

SHEEP

A good dream forecasting prosperous times.

SHEET

Receiving a surprise gift.

SHELF

Try not to be too ambitious.

SHELL

Dreaming of sea-side holidays.

SOUL

A spiritual dream.

SPEEDING

Slow down or your life will get out of control.

SPELL

Perhaps you need advice and this seems to be your only option.

SPIDER'S WEB

The old saying of 'what a tangled web we weave when first we practice to deceive' applies here.

This is an indication that you should try to stay on the straight and narrow.

SPOONS

Love surrounds you.

STAGE

A dislike of being in the spotlight.

STAIN

Someone will be spreading gossip about you.

STAIRS

If climbing the stairs, you will achieve your dreams.

Going downstairs, unfortunately, you will fail.

STAR

Harmony.

STING

Be careful. Someone has got it in for you.

STONES

If the stones were being thrown, someone will be hurling verbal abuse at you.

STORMS

Relationship troubles.

SUGAR

A sweet tooth depicts you as a good reliable person.

SUMMER

Changes for the good will be happening in the summer.

SUNGLASSES

Hiding from life is not going to solve your problems.

SUPERNATURAL
An interest in mystical happenings.

SURGEON
Professional advice will be taken in the near future.

SURGERY
Professional advice will be taken in the near future.

SWEAT
Worry, stress.
A real need is shown here to de-stress yourself.

SWIMMING
Could be that you see swimming as a way of leaving your troubles behind.
Unfortunately, this attitude will only perpetuate your troubles.

T

TABLE TENNIS
A shared pastime.
The need for more order in your life.

TANDEM
Distrust surrounds you.

TEA
Comfort.

TEACHER
A need arises for you to take professional advice.

TEETH
Hearing of a death.

TELEPHONE
A need for you to communicate with someone.

TEMPER

This dream is telling you to get all the anger out of your system.

TENT

Hiding from situations.

TEST

Stop testing yourself in all aspects of your life.

THERMOS

Feeling as if you're being ill-treated.

THIEF

Freedom from stress.

THREADS

If tangled, you need protection from yourself.

Smooth, life improves.

TICKET

Freedom.

Permission will be granted for something you want.

TIDE

An emotional time in the near future.

TIMBER

Seeking a firm friendship, i.e. someone to lean on.

TIMETABLE

A warning to put your life in order.

TISSUES

Wiping the slate clean.

TOAST

Warmth, security.

TOLLS

Unpleasant decisions will have to be made.

TOMORROW

Ahead of yourself.

Slow down.

TONGUE

Gossip surrounds you.

TOOLS

Work offers.

TORCH

Helping out someone who has relationship problems.

TORTOISE

Only you can help yourself.

TOURING

It could be predicting a holiday.

TOWING

Someone will give you a helping hand.

TOWEL

Trying to erase your troubles.

TOWER

Alteration to plans.

TOWN

Possible move.

TOYS

Perhaps you need to put aside more time for hobbies.

TRACKS

Searching for something.

TRACTOR

Plans made now will bear fruit in the autumn.

TRAFFIC

If the traffic was busy, a warning to slow-down.

If the traffic was slow, it shows you are achieving your ambitions, albeit slower than you expected.

TRAIN

Journeys will be made soon.

TRAMP

Having a low opinion of yourself, i.e. more confidence needed.

U

UMBRELLA

Hiding from the truth.

V

VACUUMING

Making a clean sweep of your life.

VALET

Someone will be offering to help you out of a difficult situation.

W

WADING

Problems will be resolved, but slower than you would like.

WAITING

The issue worrying you will be resolved eventually.

WALKING

Helping someone resolve their problems.

WALL

Problems need resolving.

WAR

Hearing bad news.

WASHING

Clearing out of problems - a fresh start.

WATER

A need to revaluate your life.

WAX

Protecting yourself from another's poison tongue.

WEAVING

Fate, karma; life goes on regardless of what happens along the way.

WEDDING

Happiness

WEEDS

One or two fresh starts for a family member.

WEEPING

Sad times ahead for the family.

WET

Worrying times ahead.

WHEAT

Ambitions realised.

WHEEL

A new beginning.

WISH

Fulfilled

WITCHES

You will feel tempted to do the wrong thing.

WIZARD

News to do with youngsters.

WOLF
You will be reorganising your life in every aspect.
WOMAN
Travel.
Tide turning in your favour.

X

X-RAY
Feeling better.

Y

YACHT
Feeling overworked. Perhaps this is a sign that you need to take time out.

Z

ZEBRA
Good times ahead.

I believe that certain dreams do predict the future. From my own point of view, I feel it is a pity that the predictive dreams that foretell disasters are not taken seriously when they are reported to the authorities. Perhaps if the authorities took note then some tragedies might be avoided. Who knows in future years things might alter when attitudes change.

ADVICE ON GIVING READINGS

To be able to give readings, you need to have a lot of patience and be a caring person. It is really important that you are a good listener. Be aware that a reading cannot be restricted to thirty minutes or an hour. Some of your customers will need to spend a long time with you. Occasionally, a visiting client isn't that interested in having a reading as such, they will just want to talk. You must always state that you aren't a professional counsellor, unless you are, of course. Always be warm and welcoming when your client arrives.

If more than one person is coming for a reading, keep the other person in a separate room with a magazine or book to occupy them when possible. A lot of personal information is given in a reading, and it's best to keep it private. You need to concentrate on the person who you are reading for and not have any other distractions.

Unless it's impossible, it is best if children are kept away from readings. Readings can take quite a long time and even a few minutes can become boring to a child, but the person having the reading needs to concentrate on what is going on and not worry about their child.

Ensure you have a notepad and pen handy, the client may want to write down what you tell them, or ask you to make notes for them.

If you are going to do psychometry as part of a reading, then a pen and pad are essential. A lot of information is received when you do a reading this way, and it is best to write it down immediately before you forget it. Should you receive anything too personal, you can avoid passing this on to the client if you feel it will upset them.

You can tape the reading, of course, but I always found this too distracting. I also worried in case the tape didn't record. I much preferred writing everything down. It might take a little longer, but it is well worth it.

Offer your visitor a cup of tea, coffee, or other refreshment. Not alcohol, as it's not a very professional approach.

Ensure the room where you are giving the reading is light, warm, bright, airy, and most of all, welcoming. Don't have fresh flowers in the room or lighted candles. I say this in case your client suffers from asthma or allergies. Silk flowers would be more appropriate. Try to avoid having any loud colours on show. The room needs to give out a calm and relaxed atmosphere. Ensure your client has a comfortable place to sit, and more importantly that they can see you properly. It's quite appropriate to have soothing music playing in the background. Nothing too loud though, certainly not rap, or anything too modern. Try to give the reading at a time when you know the house will be quiet. Switch the phones off and politely ask your client to do this as well. The less distractions you have, the better. If you have a dog, ensure he has been toileted before your customer arrives. Always have a box of tissues to hand.

This might sound strange but it is important the person having the reading can see your face while you are doing the reading. If you are reading cards, the client will want to see the card spread you are using. Some like to question you about the different cards and the meanings of them.

If you are a smoker, always ask if your customer is all right with you having a cigarette. Yes, they are on your premises, but they may well be allergic to smoke or suffer from asthma. Alternatively, they might simply dislike the smell of smoke on their clothes.

Make certain you don't frown or pull a face while you are doing a reading. Remember, your client is watching your every expression, if they see you frown or pull any sort of face, they will immediately think you have seen something awful in their reading. This will frighten them. Even if you haven't seen anything untoward in their reading, they won't believe you, however hard you try and reassure them.

It is a wise reader who doesn't mention death, serious illness, or anything too negative when giving a reading, even if they see it. For every good thing that you tell a person who you are reading for, they will only remember the one negative thing you tell them. Ninety-nine per cent of the people who go for a reading have probably been through a bad time. They want to hear good things, not bad. It is all right, in my opinion, to talk about the mundane things that show in the cards. The most important thing you should do is give the client something good and positive to look forward to. The cards will indicate when this will happen.

You must be non-judgemental and extremely trustworthy. Never ever divulge what a client tells you or what you see in their reading. Above all else, you need to respect their dignity and confidences. If you ever tell anyone what one of your clients has told you confidentially, then you will lose your self-respect and never again be trusted by clients. You will lose custom through idle gossip, word spreads fast.

Even if you disagree with your customer's point of view or actions, it's best to keep silent. You can say what your approach to any given situation might be at some time during the conversation, but it is up to the person having the reading what action they eventually take. Whatever type of reading you are offering the person, remember to tell them that you are giving them possibilities that will be presented to them in the future. It will be their choice which pathway they choose to take.

Occasionally, a client will be upset and break down in tears. In this situation, remain calm and in control, try to be comforting and reassuring. Remember, their tears are probably a release of long-held emotion, crying will help them. Once the person has stopped, more than likely they will be embarrassed by their breakdown, again be reassuring, offer a drink of water, tea, coffee, but definitely not alcohol. If they smoke and you don't object, tell them it's all right with you if they want a cigarette. If they want to talk about what's bothering them, listen patiently. Remember that this will help them tremendously as it will be a release for them along with the tears.

Most people who come for readings have emotional troubles, these are normally relationships or money troubles; of course, there are lots of other reasons that people come for readings, but the above are two of the main ones.

Don't let your clients become reliant on you for readings. I rarely saw people more than once in six months. Unfortunately, there are some people who will give people a reading every week or so. This is bad as the customer becomes dependent not only on the cards or whatever method they are using, but also on the reader. The customer must be shown that the cards are a pointer, and they have to live their own lives and make their own decisions.

If a client presents with a serious problem, don't be afraid to point them in the right direction, be it to see a lawyer, financial expert, doctor, or marriage guidance. You won't lose their custom as they will remember you as the person who gave them good advice.

Keep a list of agencies, phone numbers, opening

hours, and web addresses. If a client seems particularly distressed, point them to a good counsellor.

This might sound strange, but also keep a list of other clairvoyants and mediums who you know are good. Your clients will appreciate it.

As far as fees go, I suggest you ring around and find out what other clairvoyants in your area are charging and then settle on your own fee. Try to keep your fee as reasonable as possible so that people can afford to visit you. Never look on your work as a money spinner; your gift will quickly disappear.

You will also be invited to do group sittings. If you see more than two people at any one time, then obviously you aren't going to be able to devote much time to the readings. You must explain this to the person who books the sittings. Try not to have too many people at any one group sitting. If you do overbook yourself, you will find that you are unable to give a satisfactory reading as you will have to rush. Again, explain this to the client.

You can work out the type of reading that you give to group bookings. You can select quick readings rather than the normal in-depth readings that you offer. As long as the clients are aware of this, then you can press ahead without feeling as if you haven't done your best. I would suggest you do a three-month reading and a six-month reading followed by either a reading from the crystal ball or psychometry. Give your client the choice.

You will find that people from every walk of life will visit you for readings. Treat every single person the same.

Whatever job they may do, from doctor to bank manager to cleaners, always remember we all have the same emotions. We all fall in love, we all get hurt, we all get ill at some time or other, and unfortunately through life. we lose our relatives and friends. The pain we experience is the same for all of us.

KEEP YOURSELF SAFE

It is important that you keep yourself secure when you are working alone. Unfortunately, in today's society where drink and drugs abound, a reader can be an easy target. It is essential that you put safeguards in place.

If possible, always ensure that there is someone else in the house with you when you are giving a reading, day or night.

Consider having a personal alarm about your person. Don't switch your mobile phone off; just turn it to silent mode so you have immediate access to it. Have one of those doorbells that sound as if there is a dog in the house.

A dog offers protection, if you own one (all the better if it's big), take it to the door with you. If the client doesn't object and your dog is well trained, keep it beside you whilst the reading is in progress. I used to do this with my dogs when I gave readings. It certainly made me feel safer.

If possible, work near a window and the front or back door.

Always imply that there is someone else in the house

with you. Never say 'I', say 'we'. It gives the impression you aren't alone.

MOBILE READERS

Don't go out to a stranger's house alone, take someone with you.

Obviously, if you know the person who has booked you to visit them, that's fine.

If a stranger invites you to their home to give a group reading, it is up to you to check them out first. Pay them a visit with a friend. It is important that you don't visit them alone. Whilst at their house, check that the room where you will do the reading is satisfactory. You don't want to find yourself in a pokey, dark, cold room. Make certain there is a table and a couple of chairs, and that you will be warm and comfortable. Give clear details of how long each reading will take, and of your charges. In fact, it is a good idea to give the party holder a list of how you work.

Remember to tell your hostess your arrival time, ensure you will have a parking space, and your approximate time of leaving.

Before leaving for the group sitting, check you have your cards or whatever method you are going to use. Notepad and pen, or tape recorder (with batteries or plug). A box of tissues, essential for yourself and possibly your clients. If people are going to pay you separately, ensure you have plenty of change. Unless you know the person who is paying you, it isn't a good idea to accept a cheque. Have your business card to pass on should anyone wish to contact you at a later date or to pass on your details to a friend. Ensure your mobile phone is fully charged.

Take a torch in case your car breaks down. Don't forget your mobile and alarm. Ensure you have enough fuel in your car and that it's recently been serviced. Keep a warm blanket in the back of the car in case you break down.

If you have followed all the things I have mentioned, the only thing left to say is enjoy your evening.

At some point, you may well be invited to give talks about your work. If you decide to accept, remember to be professional at all times and never disclose anything about any clients that you have seen or heard. This is important no matter how far away from where you gave the reading you happen to be. There will always be someone who recognises the person you are talking about. To illustrate any point you may wish to talk about, you can make up a reading and also an imaginary client. This is far better than being unprofessional. Anything you have heard or seen in a reading is strictly confidential between you and your client.

PSYCHIC FAIRS

In my opinion, psychic fairs aren't exactly the best venue to give readings. I know they are popular and that a lot of money can be made. Personally, I feel it is next to impossible to concentrate on a client in such a busy and noisy environment. I know I could never do readings at such places.

If you decide this is the way for you to work, then remember the days can be very long and you, as well your cards, will become 'tired'. It might be wise to buy at least four new decks of cards (if that's what you use) to take along with you, and ensure you take plenty of breaks.

SUMMING UP

When the psychic journey begins it is very exciting and as new ideas are tried whole new worlds begin to open up.

I feel it is up to an individual to make their own minds up which path they choose to follow. I know I appreciated the fact that I received invaluable advice along the way, but no one ever tried to force me along a path that wasn't of my choosing. Most people who are involved in the psychic world understand the need for people to make their own choices as to which path they wish to follow.

Care must be taken at all times where the paranormal is concerned. Never take what you are told as gospel. Stand back and research the subject thoroughly, and then make your own judgement; you will be able to avoid the pitfalls more easily. As I have pointed out earlier, there are certain things I disagree with regarding the paranormal, but this doesn't mean that they are wrong. It's purely my view.

I do believe in many of the psychic crafts - not all, I

might add - but it's not for me to say which ones you should avoid. I wouldn't like to cloud anyone else's judgement.

I hope my explanations are an aid to anyone interested in following the psychic pathway. Obviously, whichever one is pursued, the individual person will eventually put their own interpretations on to the craft they choose.